TEACHING EUROPEAN STUDIES

Teaching
European Studies

MICHAEL WILLIAMS

*Department of Education,
University of Manchester*

HEINEMANN EDUCATIONAL BOOKS

Heinemann Educational Books Ltd

LONDON   EDINBURGH   MELBOURNE   AUCKLAND   TORONTO
HONG KONG   SINGAPORE   KUALA LUMPUR
IBADAN   NAIROBI   JOHANNESBURG
LUSAKA   NEW DELHI   KINGSTON

Cased edition ISBN 0 435 80920 2
Paper edition ISBN 0 435 80921 0

Published by Heinemann Educational Books Ltd
48 Charles Street, London W1X 8AH
Printed in Great Britain by
Biddles Ltd, Guildford, Surrey

Contents

Preface

In writing this short book I have sought to inform and stimulate discussion among teachers and student teachers of European Studies in secondary schools. Throughout the following pages the predominant emphasis will be upon those European Studies courses designed for pupils taking examinations for the Certificate of Secondary Education as this clearly reflects the area of the curricula of secondary schools in which teachers have been most actively engaged in developing courses.

This book is the product of my experience in trying to teach the subject in secondary schools, in training student teachers to teach European Studies courses, in discussing these courses with teachers on many in-service courses, and particularly in moderating CSE Mode 3 European Studies courses in schools in north-west England. This experience has convinced me that European Studies courses represent a valuable curriculum innovation and that when competently taught these courses have considerable potential for extending the horizons of secondary school pupils beyond their local and national environments. If pupils can understand some of the most important aspects of the life of the continent in which they live they are likely to transfer their understanding and modes of study to other countries and continents. European Studies are not background studies, they are foreground studies; they are a means to an end, and that end is improved international understanding.

By their very nature European Studies courses are integrated studies, drawing on a number of disciplines for content, skills and modes of study. They are difficult courses to teach and learn. In these courses teachers have found that they must modify their teaching strategies and alter their relationships with teachers in other departments in schools. Pupils frequently find non-language studies much more difficult than studies of a modern language.

Because European Studies courses are usually based on the contemporary European scene teachers are forced to rely more and more on resources other than the traditional school textbook. The courses may be expensive to mount in terms of time and money. Experience indicates that they cannot be introduced successfully without considerable thought and planning.

In a decade when the Schools Council through its curriculum development projects has given much support, stimulation and encouragement to teachers in virtually all school subjects, European Studies courses have been unusual in that they have been generated predominantly by local initiatives. A few pioneering teachers have been able to contribute to the activities of organized groups of their colleagues and from these nuclei other groups have benefited. European Studies courses are a good example of the 'grass roots' tradition of British curriculum innovation, a tradition which produces curricular variety. In discussing European Studies this variety must always be kept to the fore. Thus, I am conscious that my interpretation must inevitably be personal. If I had been a specialist in, say, modern languages, this would have been a quite different book; my perspective is largely that of the geographer interested in interdisciplinary courses and I see in European Studies courses the possibility of integrating a modern language into a humanities course focusing upon a single continent. In the early years of the development of European Studies in schools this integration has proved to be exceptionally difficult: it is certainly the challenge for the future.

Some readers may be disappointed or surprised that there is hardly a reference to French or German Studies in this book. The exclusion of discussion of these courses is intentional. While it would appear logical to include 'background' or 'civilisation' studies within modern language courses such studies focusing on a single country would appear to have little merit when the language element is dropped. Unless *all* the pupils in a school class will visit the country chosen for study it is difficult to see why extended studies of a single European country should be promoted.

In focusing upon European Studies *courses* as such one should not forget the long tradition within the development of the British secondary school curriculum of teaching about Europe. Clearly many school subjects include references to aspects of European culture and there are some educationists who would wish to see all school subjects given a European dimension. While it is not the purpose of this book to consider this dimension, I would argue that teachers of all subjects should be sensitive to the potential of their subjects for promoting international awareness and I would see European Studies as an important stepping stone in that direction. If European Studies courses can be mounted successfuly then they may eventually be seen as a great stride towards effective world studies courses.

The opening chapter of this book offers explanations as to why European Studies courses have been introduced into schools. They are a new feature of secondary schools and are becoming increasingly common. When teachers meet to discuss European Studies the two problems which preoccupy them are the place of modern languages in courses and the limits of the region on which studies focus. These two problems are the subject of the second chapter. How these problems have been resolved in the design of courses is indicated in Appendix A where five course outlines are quoted in detail. Translating syllabuses into teachable courses is the problem facing teachers preparing candidates for examinations and early decisions have to be made regarding staffing and the organization of teachers for the courses. Integrated courses and team teaching are the two themes discussed in Chapter 3. The success of any school course must finally be judged on what the pupils have learned by the end of a course. It is to be hoped that at the end of a European Studies course pupils will be able to solve problems, that they should have formed new concepts and that their attitudes may have changed. These aspects of learning are dealt with in Chapter 4.

Teaching strategies in European Studies rely to a great extent upon those subjects which have been integrated to form the new courses. It is argued in Chapter 5 that the study visit to a mainland European country is the most distinctive aspect of European Studies teaching. The potential for European Studies of enquiry-based, individualized learning and of simulations and educational games is also considered.

In Chapter 6 nine themes commonly encountered in European Studies courses are broken down into concept networks since these indicate how topics may be linked and how various school subjects may contribute to courses. By listing key questions related to the themes it is possible to define the aims which it is hoped to accomplish in school classrooms. Guidance is given as to books which should help teachers in preparing for teaching the themes. How the themes can be linked together to form a teaching course is dealt with in this chapter. From teaching schemes the next step would logically appear to be the single lesson and so in Chapter 7 three different kinds of European Studies lessons are described.

Throughout the preceding chapters there are many references to school examinations and especially to the Certificate of Secondary Education. In Chapter 8 consideration is given to the processes of moderation of CSE Mode 3 courses and to the techniques of examining pupils.

In the Conclusion the major themes discussed in the book are summarized and an attempt is made to assess the possible future of European Studies courses in schools.

I should like to express my gratitude to Robert Wilson, now Deputy Head of Nether Stowe Comprehensive School, Lichfield, and formerly Sixth Form Tutor at New Mills Comprehensive School, and Susan Butter, Deputy Head at Poynton High School and formerly Head of Modern Languages, who allowed me to teach their pupils and in our many lengthy discussions taught me valuable lessons about how teachers with training in ancient or modern languages viewed Europe and European Studies. John McNair, a colleague in the Department of Education, read the manuscript and made many constructive suggestions for which I am especially grateful. In thinking about examinations in European Studies I owe much to my colleagues Sheila Beeden and Gordon Kilner with whom I have worked on CSE European Studies courses for several years.

Michael Williams, 1977

Acknowledgements

I am grateful to the following for permission to reproduce syllabuses and published materials: Mr. B. King, County Adviser for Languages, Somerset County Council; Mr. L. W. Owain, European Studies Adviser, Oxfordshire County Council; Mr. J. A. Day, Deputy Secretary, The Associated Examining Board; Mr. J. E. Tipping, Secretary, North West Regional Examinations Board; Mr. H. B. Ellis, Headmaster, Up Holland Grammar School, Up Holland; Miss D. W. Preston, Headmistress, Blacon High School, Blacon, Chester; Mrs. P. Knowles, Adviser, Hillingdon; Mr. R. A. Wake, Staff Inspector, Department of Education and Science.

Part I

Aims and Organization

CHAPTER ONE

Why European Studies?

Courses bearing the title European Studies are newcomers to the British curricular scene. In seeking to explain their emergence it is possible to consider two different approaches: firstly we can examine the conditions in which European Studies have been initiated in schools, and secondly we can look at the statements of aims and objectives which are commonly an integral part of course outlines.

Conditions conducive to the introduction of European Studies courses

1   A wide sweeping review of curricula in British secondary schools supports the contention that teachers seek to impress their own individual stamp upon the courses they teach. It is a function of the degree of freedom which British teachers enjoy that courses, even those bearing traditional labels and taught by the most conventional methods, are strikingly different in their organizational and teaching characteristics from teacher to teacher and from school to school. Any attempt to explain the emergence of new courses must begin with this acknowledgement of the scope given for teacher initiative. Similarly, the variety of courses bearing numerous labels which is such a distinctive feature of contemporary school curricula may be seen as a product of the evolution of school subjects. By some teachers the curricular variety is viewed as a pathological condition: all around is seen disarray, disorganization, confusion. Others see the situation as one of constructive progress where in individual schools, teachers are utilizing their professional competence to design learning experiences appropriate for the education of their charges. Teacher individuality and experimental course design are neither new nor even recent phenomena. What is new is the amount of publicity which now accompanies experimentation and the amount of attention given to the diffusion of ideas and novel practices. Thus European Studies has grown as a national movement.

2   Changes in secondary school organization, especially comprehensive reorganization, have been accompanied by experiment in such

fields as teaching mixed ability groups, team teaching and integrated studies. These innovations are most frequently provided for pupils in the eleven-to-thirteen age-group and they represent attempts by schools to provide 'equal opportunities' for children of diverse abilities.

This development can be seen in terms of the curriculum. Some educational theorists have distinguished between the Classical and Romantic views of the curriculum and Lawton (1973) has summarized the division between these in two lists:

Classical	*Romantic*
Subject-centred	Child-centred
Skills	Creativity
Instruction	Experience
Information	Discovery
Obedience	Awareness
Conformity	Originality
Discipline	Freedom

Applying this simplified dichotomy to the curriculum more closely, Lawton draws up this arrangement:

Classical	*Romantic*
Objectives	Processes
Acquiring knowledge	'Living' attitudes and values
Content	Experiences
Subjects	Real-life topics and projects
Method	Method
Didactic instruction	Involvement
Competition	Co-operation
Evaluation	Evaluation
By tests (teacher-set) and	Self-assessment (in terms
examinations (public and	of self-improvement)
competitive)	

A careful reading of Chapters 3 and 4 will show the extent to which European Studies courses embody many of the characteristics classified under the heading *Romantic*. In the chapters concerned with learning and teaching the tensions between the two ideologies become evident.

3   Teacher individuality, subject evolution and the attractiveness of the romantic ideology have contributed to the development of courses which derive their subject matter from the broad field of the humanities. Evidence of this can be witnessed in the sixth-form field of general studies, in the social studies movement of the immediate post-war years and in the more recent experimentation in courses labelled humanities, in the expansion of liberal studies courses in

colleges of further education, and in the progress made in developing social studies and environmental studies courses in primary schools. These arrangements contain two significant growth points for European Studies. First, the emphasis on applying to school courses study methods derived from the social sciences; second, the focusing of studies upon man and his place in society and more particularly upon contemporary man and society. Later in this chapter these two elements provide important threads running through the quoted statements of course aims and objectives and they appear again even more noticeably in the detailed course outlines quoted in Appendix A. In the succeeding chapters it becomes more and more evident that European Studies courses are an integral part of what Lawton and Dufour (1973) have termed 'the Social Studies Movement'.

4   Associated with teacher individuality and the design of new courses has been experimentation with new forms of pupil assessment. For European Studies as for other new courses the introduction of school-based, externally-moderated examinations for school leavers, through the CSE examination boards, has provided the means whereby pupils have been able to obtain paper qualifications at the end of their studies while at the same time contributing to making European Studies courses 'respectable' in the eyes of parents, employers and other teachers not involved in the teaching of these courses. Without the CSE examinations, and especially the Mode 3 arrangements it is most unlikely that the study of European Studies would have achieved the progress which it has. Courses have evolved very largely within the patterns acceptable to CSE examination boards. This is a point to which we return many times in later chapters and it justifies the space given to CSE examinations in Chapter 8.

5   No discussion of changes in curriculum and examinations can ignore the part played by the Schools Council since it began work in 1964. Through reports and the activities of the curriculum development projects the Schools Council has made an enormous contribution to the diffusion of new ideas and innovative practices referred to earlier. Although the Schools Council has not given support to any curriculum development project labelled European Studies (though proposals for such projects have been submitted without success) there have been spin-off effects for the teaching of European Studies derived from other projects. In particular the Integrated Studies Project, the Humanities Curriculum Project, and the General Studies Project have, through their publications, in-service courses and other dissemination activities, given European Studies enthusiasts exemplars of work which can be modified for use in their classrooms. It is no easy task to determine the degree of influence which Schools Council activities have had upon European Studies courses in general or in particular. Where there are

obvious connections these have been highlighted in the discussion about courses in later chapters.

6   Although the Schools Council has contributed to the climate which permitted the emergence and evolution of European Studies courses its influence has been felt most by practising teachers. For the student teacher the universities, polytechnics and colleges of higher education have been an important influence. These institutions have also experimented with new courses of European Studies and have produced graduates with new and original academic backgrounds. The entry of many of these graduates into secondary schools has provided much of the impetus for the European Studies movement. The introduction of new business studies courses with a significant modern language component and new modern language degree courses with complements to language studies derived from social, political and economic fields, are also important. Graduates from these courses who become teachers are often eager to impart their new knowledge and experience to school pupils. In Chapter 3 some attention is paid to the models of European Studies course organization which are found in institutions of higher education some of which have influenced schools. The parallel evolution of European Studies courses at various levels of the educational system has been important in leading to the introduction of increasing numbers of these courses in schools.

7   Another important contribution has been the work of several agencies which are, for various reasons, especially concerned with promoting consciousness of Europe in Britain's teachers and pupils. The most influential of these agencies are the Schools Information Unit of the Centre for Contemporary European Studies at the University of Sussex,* the European Atlantic Movement (TEAM), the European Schools Day Movement, the European Communities Information Service, the European Association of Teachers, the Atlantic Information Centre for Teachers and the Council of Europe's Centre for Cultural Co-operation. The addresses of these organizations can be found in Appendix B.

Details of their activities, and those of other organizations, are listed in the annual publication of the Department of Education and Science, *Sources of Information on International Organisations*. All these agencies produce publications, organize conferences and generally encourage teachers to give some attention to European themes in their school courses. They support activities organized in teachers' centres and teacher-training institutions by inspectors, local authority advisers and teacher-training tutors. These activities were very prominent in 1973, the first year of Britain's membership of the European

---

*The series of Curriculum Development papers published by this Centre are highly recommended to teachers of European Studies.

Community. Through these media the debate about the pros and cons of European Studies as an educational endeavour has continued in recent years. The debate has gone on in schools, local authorities, subject associations and examination boards. It is from the agencies referred to above that most of the facts about the evolution of European Studies have been forthcoming. Many of the ideas discussed in this book have arisen from discussions promoted by these agencies and from information derived from their publications.

8 It is unlikely that European Studies courses would have developed in the way that they have if international political circumstances had been different. On the one hand, there is little doubt that there were post-war pressures to educate children to know Europeans better in the hope of avoiding future hostility. Outbreaks of violence, such as those in Hungary, Czechoslovakia, France, Cyprus, Greece, Portugal and Northern Ireland have also focused the attention of teachers and their pupils upon the European scene. In this context the impact of the mass media, especially television documentaries and news broadcasts, upon adolescents' and teachers' perceptions of Europe must be taken into consideration. On the other hand, the movement towards political and economic unity in western Europe has been an important component of the cultural backcloth of the British educational scene in post-war years. This movement, combined with the more recent steps towards *détente* between eastern and western Europe, has been paralleled by social and cultural changes. These include not only an increase in sporting, aesthetic and mass-media interchanges but also in the movement of Europeans of all ages on their continent in numbers which increase annually. These changes have obviously impressed themselves upon schools. One of the more promising features of the development of European Studies courses is the broadening of the base of school visits and the stimulus given to inter-disciplinary study visits to mainland Europe. In terms of both syllabus content and teaching methods the influence of these political changes can be seen in European Studies courses (see the course examples quoted in Appendix A).

With such a wide variety of conditions influencing the development of courses it is not surprising that as we shall see later in Chapter 3 there is such a diversity of course arrangements in European Studies. Mediating between the syllabuses and the conditions already described are the aims and objectives which have been formulated for the courses.

Aims

At the outset we must acknowledge the difficulties which teachers encounter in distinguishing between aims and objectives. It is usual to distinguish between the word 'aims' which is utilized to define a general and abstract level of purpose and the word 'objectives' which is used in a much more specific way, as Bloom and Krathwohl (1956) have written: 'By educational objectives we mean explicit formulations of the ways in which students are expected to be changed by the educative process. That is, the ways they will change in their thinking, their feelings and their actions'. Teachers are obliged to make these distinctions by the requirements of examinations boards when they submit course proposals for validation. Details of this procedure are given in Chapter 8. For the moment we can focus on the formulation of aims and notice the way these aims have been influenced by the conditions already outlined.

The aims of European Studies courses can be grouped under four broad headings: social, cultural, political, and vocational. The divisions between these four groups are arbitrary and the groups themselves receive different degrees of emphasis from individual teachers.

Under the heading 'social' the principal aim is the promotion of 'social awareness' which has become a curriculum slogan used to cover all those aspects of teaching which lead to an improved understanding by the adolescent of himself and his role or roles in society. While this has a narrow definition in terms of socialization theories, for the European Studies teacher it takes on the rather special meaning of broadening the child's social horizon to encompass individuals and groups from various parts of Europe. It is both child-centred and society-centred education. The aim of social awareness incorporates improved international understanding, which in contemporary historical terms grows directly from the last item in the list of conditions conducive to the introduction of European Studies courses already discussed. Education for international understanding has long been a fundamental aim of British education and European Studies courses serve to pinpoint the European perspective. Social awareness also incorporates the aim of education for leisure. In a European Studies context this presupposes that increasing numbers of pupils will, while they are at school and later when they are adults, be sufficiently affluent to spend some of their leisure time on mainland Europe. It also means that more and more people even if they do not travel in Europe will learn to enjoy such expressions of European life as food, sport and the arts. A study of European Studies syllabuses submitted to a CSE examinations board produces these examples of social aims:

To prepare pupils for future European visits and exchanges.
To seek to increase international goodwill with special reference to European societies.
To study some of the social, economic and cultural features of

Europe, as well as its history and geography and, by stressing similarities in our ways of life and heritage, to make the pupil conscious of being a European.

To create an awareness of the similarities and differences between European countries to develop understanding and tolerance.

To introduce the pupils to the varying ways of life of our European neighbours by comparing aspects of these with each other and with our own, and thus to develop an understanding of different environments, traditions and aspirations of the European peoples.

The last example illustrates the difficulty of distinguishing between social and cultural aims. The division has been made principally as a result of discussions with teachers of modern languages who tend to associate the word 'culture' with those topics which added together constitute 'background studies' or 'civilization' in modern language courses. Broadly, it is the area which Raymond Williams seems to have in mind when, in defining the five minimum requirements to aim at for the educationally normal child, he gave as one of his items 'introduction to at least one other culture, including its language, history, geography, institutions and arts, to be given in part by visiting and exchanges' (Williams, R. 1961). Examples of cultural aims quoted in European Studies courses include:

To stimulate interest in and develop understanding of the ways of life of European countries and their peoples.

To outline the origin and development of the arts in Europe comprising mainly a study of ideas in painting, sculpture, architecture and music, but touching also on literature, theatre and other arts.

To assess the role and importance of the arts in contemporary European life.

To outline the origin and development of the main European language groups, to indicate their inter-relationships and to consider the possibility of a universal language for Europe.

To compare and contrast from a thematic point of view aspects of contemporary Europe as a whole, discussing the origins, influences and possible consequences. Themes include: industrial relations, habits, customs and traditions, press and broadcasting, food and the consumer, prejudice and hostility, leisure and sport, women in Europe, youth in Europe.

Political aims emphasize the new concept of citizenship which membership of international organizations brings to the citizens of member states. Citizens must be informed of their citizens' rights and duties particularly in Britain with regard to the European Community and the school is considered by some to be the most important agency available to transmit this information. It is in the statements of political aims of European Studies courses that we can see some of the links between the movement towards political unification in western Europe and the agencies active in promoting a European consciousness among schoolchildren. These examples of quoted aims serve to illustrate this:

To create an awareness of Britain's role in Europe.

To give a brief historical outline of Europe from its early origins taking as a theme 'European Unity' and tracing those events and developments which have influenced the unity or disunity of the European nations with emphasis on the contemporary situation. To show further how the individual political, economic, social and cultural characteristics of European nations have arisen, leading to a growing realisation of the advantages of unity in a world of political and economic blocs.

To observe economic and other forces which have determined Europe's position as a leading industrialized continent and to consider the inter-relationship between the European economic blocs and the rest of the world and the likely consequences of this in the future.

To study post-war movements which have promoted economic, social and political unity in Europe as a whole including various crises and flashpoints which have had wide repercussions.

To show the need for European peoples to work in harmony for the common good and the way the EEC has worked and is working to that end.

To arouse and develop an interest in the European world in which the pupil can participate as an informed citizen.

Vocational aims rarely figure in lists of aims for school courses in European Studies. They appear to be more relevant to courses taught in colleges of further education, polytechnics and universities. At this level they focus on the improved career prospects for school leavers and more especially graduates from higher education wishing to find employment in Europe and the increasing contact between British and other European nationals in all spheres of work.

'

Objectives
At the end of this chapter we shall return to aims when two examples of lists of aims and objectives taken from two school courses are quoted at length. Before that it is necessary to consider the way in which aims, such as those quoted above, can be put into practice. Defining specific objectives is a first step in achieving this.

While the writing of lists of specific objectives is not a popular activity for teachers the demands of examination boards and the encouragement given through curriculum development projects of various kinds have produced statements of objectives. The most important stimulus to the elucidation of objectives was given by the publication of detailed classified lists (taxonomies) by Bloom and his co-workers (Bloom 1956) in the United States. Here we find objectives divided into three major groups: cognitive objectives, affective objectives and objectives associated with the learning of skills. The last defines itself. Cognitive objectives focus upon pupils' abilities to recall knowledge in the same form as it was learned and affective objectives relate to the learning of attitudes, values and understandings. Within each of the three groups there are, in Bloom's writings, long lists of learned behavioural characteristics organized into hierarchical patterns from the most simple to the most difficult. There has been much academic discussion over the value of objectives and, while suspicion may be cast over the controlled teaching which might result from an over-zealous adherence to pre-ordained objectives (Stenhouse 1975) there can be little doubt that in evaluating pupil progress, teacher competence and course validity, statements of specific objectives are of crucial importance.

To illustrate how teachers of European Studies have interpreted the concept of cognitive objectives these examples taken from CSE syllabuses will serve:

To give pupils a knowledge of the basic geography of Europe; to give them an awareness of its past but more especially of developments which have occurred this century, and to help them understand the patterns of European economic, social and political life.

To be able to identify common and dissimilar features of chosen areas of study which exemplify the following: types of agriculture, the fishing industry, industry, energy and power, transport and communications, schooling.

To study the working of the EEC from the viewpoints of what it does, how it works, where the money comes from and where it goes and the history of the institution.

To recognize and identify the main frontiers, rivers, mountains, coastlines, principal towns, sea ports, agricultural and industrial regions of the six countries to be studied.

To compare local and international traditions in leisure and holiday activities.

From this brief list of examples it is clear that pupils may be asked to recall factual data for direct repetition, may be asked to make comparisons and contrasts, to recognize, identify and understand patterns and developments. Further discussion of these, and other, cognitive objectives can be found in Chapters 4, 5 and 8.

Affective objectives focusing upon values receive relatively little attention in European Studies syllabuses. Fenton (1966) has distinguished three types of values with which teachers must deal: behavioural, procedural and substantive.

A behavioural value is concerned with pupil behaviour in the classroom or other learning situation. Thus in seeking an atmosphere in which pupils will engage effectively in worthwhile educational activities the teacher is aiming at behavioural values. Such behavioural objectives as these are unlikely to figure in syllabuses though they may underlie the decision made by a school to introduce European Studies to particular pupils, e.g. pupils who demonstrate total lack of interest in the learning of, say, French, may be taught European Studies on the grounds that this may arouse their interest and motivate them to improved behaviour in school.

Procedural values are concerned mainly with the discipline of the subject area being studied. Thus accuracy of observation and description would constitute a procedural value. The following examples illustrate procedural values taken from European Studies courses:

> To weigh opposing factors and develop a well-reasoned attitude towards events and people which have affected life in Europe today.
> To form and to express by argued essays opinions on a wide variety of national and international situations and conditions.
> To unify pieces of information concerning Europe acquired in different subject disciplines.
> At the conclusion of the course pupils will be: (a) precise in observation, in recording their findings in a variety of ways and stimulated to seek explanations; (b) trained in the use and appreciation of source materials; (c) aware of Europe's problems and concerned for their solution; (d) conscious of man's changing response to his environment.

Substantive values are the least clear-cut and are subject to controversy because they are those which some people would describe as societal values. The example which Fenton quotes is 'democracy is better than totalitarianism' and he argues that while it is right for a teacher to engage in discussion of these values in the classroom he should not teach a set of such values as truth. It is to be expected that substantive values like procedural values will be left out of course descriptions. It could be argued that the introduction of a European Studies course is a concrete illustration of the application of substantive values since it might appear that 'European Studies' implies that

Europe is more worthy of study than other continents. Further, the emphases given to particular countries or regions, economic or political groupings, events or personalities, particularly periods of history, themes or topics reflect a teacher's values which may be transmitted consciously or unconsciously to the pupils.

In reading the examples of aims and objectives from European Studies courses quoted so far the reader is likely to have been struck by the apparent lack of subject uniqueness in these statements. Many of them are shared with traditional subjects and this should not be surprising when we consider that European Studies courses are integrated and they derive their content, methods of teaching and assessment from combinations of traditional subjects. This point will be examined in detail in Chapter 3. Here we need only emphasize that it is in statements about skills and abilities that shared objectives become most apparent as these examples show:

To interpret statistical data and photographic evidence.
To discuss critically extracts from books, newspapers and magazines.
To provide pupils with the means of personal development by gaining personal experience of working through research and project work.
To use a wide variety of means of expression, but especially objective essays, visual representation, argued essays, in such a way as to bring out the special significance of a topic.
To master techniques in the use of primary and secondary sources, e.g. documents, photographs, pictures, films, textbooks, television and radio broadcasts.
To give pupils useful skills in reading, listening, writing and speaking one of the major European languages.

In European Studies courses there is a noticeable emphasis upon procedural objectives such as these reflecting the recent drive in teaching which seeks in Torsten Husen's words (1974) 'to impart to the students the skill of learning how to acquire learning'.

So far we have been looking at examples of different kinds of aims and objectives. The examples have been drawn from a large number of CSE Mode 3 courses. These courses are designed as two-year courses for 14-16 year-olds. To demonstrate how aims and objectives are brought together in individual courses the following quotations are taken from two courses. The examples are quoted directly from the course proposals submitted to an examination board. Thus they were written originally to assist a moderator in reaching a decision as to whether or not the board should accept the course for examination. In discussion with the moderator it is to be expected that some of the objectives would be clarified and different emphases would be placed upon particular objectives than might be suggested by the order in which they have been written.

Example 1
Aims
1 To stimulate interest in, and develop understanding of, the ways of life of European countries and their peoples.
2 To create an awareness of the similarities and differences between European countries to develop understanding and tolerance.
3 To identify contemporary problems, attitudes and social and cultural conditions in Europe.
4 To create an awareness of the lives of the candidates' contemporaries in Europe.

Objectives
1 To extract significant points from factual information, charts, tables, etc. and to analyse and reproduce them in essay form.
2 To recognize, understand and explain the moral and social significance of problems in contemporary Europe.
3 To explain the interrelation of different social circumstances and problems and to relate them to the human situation.
4 To compare similar problems and different circumstances in different countries.
5 To form and express by argued essays opinions on a wide variety of national and international situations and conditions.
6 To use a variety of means of expression especially objective essays, visual representation, argued essays, in such a way as to bring out the special significance of a topic.
7 To choose a particular subject of interest, develop it and present it in the form of a special study.
8 To compare the political and industrial conditions in contrasting areas of Europe.
9 To compare local and international traditions in leisure and holiday activities.
10 To relate European matters to the narrower field of Britain, and to the wider field of European interests and influences in the rest of the world.

Example 2
Aims
1 To reduce insularity by promoting awareness of and interest in Europe and as wide a spectrum as possible of European ways of life, through the study of the history, geography, culture and language of its peoples.

2 To provide a background of European knowledge sufficient to aid understanding of current events on the continent.

3 To offer pupils the opportunity to study an additional foreign language at a highly practical level as a means of basic communication standard and the extraction of essential practical information.

Objectives

1 To acquire knowledge of and an interest in the major developments and trends in twentieth-century Europe as set out in the syllabus, i.e. to recall facts, to recognize the meaning of historical terms.

2 To weigh opposing factors and develop a well-reasoned attitude towards events and people which have affected life in Europe today.

3 To learn how to use primary and secondary sources, e.g. documents, photographs, pictures, films, textbooks, television and radio broadcasts.

4 To learn the causes of conflicts, how settlements and agreements are reached and to compare the ways in which nations are attempting to work towards peaceful co-existence.

5 To understand the workings of and reasons for the various European organizations which have sprung up in the post-war period.

6 To compare the economies of the various countries of Europe.

7 To understand the relation between the natural resources and government policy of a country and its economy.

8 To enable pupils to read a single passage in German, answer simple questions on everyday life, understand the gist of a conversation, take part in that conversation reasonably well and, most important of all 'get by' on a visit to Germany (grammatical accuracy is not the primary objective of the course).

9 By the end of the course it is hoped that the pupils will have learned to link Europe's past with the present and have some insight into the ways in which the continent has progressed from disunity and open hostility at the beginning of the twentieth century to its present position of mutual co-operation and *détente* between the two major political groupings.

In the brief statements of aims of both of these courses there is an emphasis upon social aims with particular reference to international understanding. The second course differs significantly from the first in its reference to modern language learning. We shall look at the place of modern languages in European Studies courses in the next chapter. In the statements of objectives there is a mixture of the cognitive, affective and the development of skills. These statements are indicative of the scope of European Studies and we can now turn to this topic.

CHAPTER TWO

The Scope of European Studies

In the last chapter four aims for European Studies courses were identified: social, cultural, political and vocational. Expressed in these terms they would appear to have little direct connection with the conventional curriculum subjects of secondary schools and yet, guided by the statements of objectives quoted earlier, it is from such subjects as geography, history, economics and modern languages that we would expect the subject matter for study to be derived. The reading of course syllabuses and course outlines which have been prepared to help in the design of syllabuses confirms that this expectation is fulfilled. In Appendix A examples of such syllabuses and course outlines have been quoted in their entirety and the reader who has little or no experience of teaching European Studies is well advised to read through them now since there will be several references made to them in the ensuing pages. This chapter will concentrate on the substantive areas from which European Studies courses are drawn.

As was suggested at the start of Chapter 1 European Studies courses are one of the products of the relative freedom teachers in England and Wales have to initiate new courses in school curricula. Courses of this kind grow out of existing subjects which is not surprising because secondary school teachers are recruited to contribute to the development of existing subjects. In European Studies it is possible to trace the evolution of such courses through the changes taking place within particular schools in one or two subjects. Thus in some comprehensive secondary schools teachers originally recruited to teach French or German are sometimes found teaching courses labelled French Studies or German Studies in which the traditional background or civilization studies have become their primary concern and the modern language component may have moved from foreground to background or ceased to exist altogether. The step from French to French Studies (without French) would appear to be an enormous step for a trained linguist. The step from French Studies to European Studies which increasing numbers of linguists are making would appear to be a relatively small one. It is the agonizing of modern linguists about the place of modern languages in courses of European Studies which is one of the most distinctive features of their development.

Modern Languages and European Studies

Undoubtedly the strongest arguments for making a modern language element a basic ingredient in any European Studies course have come from the Somerset Standing Committee for European Studies. An article by King (1974) summarizes the case. He argues that a modern language element should be included in a European Studies course designed for the 'lower and below CSE candidate' for three reasons:

(a) 'the regrettable dearth of suitable language courses for the less able';

(b) the desirability of bringing 'the language element if possible into line with the movement towards integration, making of it a tool to service other areas in the syllabus';

(c) the need to devise a language element which would enable more of the pupils travelling to mainland Europe 'to derive real benefit from these study-visits and which might help to increase the number and range of pupils able to undertake them'.

His argument is based on the assumption that 'lower and below CSE candidates' benefit from the inclusion of a modern language study in their curricula. The case for such an inclusion was stated in the Newsom Report (Central Advisory Committee for Education 1963) and it rests on three tenets:

(a) 'Learning to speak in a foreign tongue offers one more experience of the significance of words as tools, as means of indicating particular objects or actions or ideas; and as a result of this, though very simply in the case of the more limited pupils, they may begin to think about the use of words in their own language'.

(b) Most importantly, 'the learning of a new language may give confidence to those pupils who need it most—the less than average, those who have had difficulty with English'. Through learning a modern language it is argued a pupil will gain in self-respect and will acquire an improved attitude to learning.

(c) Learning a modern language, especially if associated with a foreign study-visit supplemented by reading about the country in question, provides 'a window on the world, a chance to extend their experience through contact with a different people and culture'.

The overall case stems from the experience of teachers in secondary modern schools. In the Newsom Survey schools 'just under a third of the modern schools provided some foreign language teaching, mainly in French and largely confined to the ablest pupils'. Later the report quotes the successful experience of teaching a foreign language to girls from all levels of ability in a comprehensive school. The authors of the Newsom Report 'would not deny even to the least able the privilege and the fun of being able to say a few simple things in a language other than their own'.

Many European Studies courses have begun with the feeling of modern language teachers that a small 'pill' of language will be taken by weak pupils if it is strongly dissolved in a heavy surfeit of jam, i.e. non-language study. When Neather asserts (1973) 'As the first article of faith may I say that a language is an essential element of the European Studies course' he quickly qualifies this by emphasizing that the course must be tied to a study-visit to a foreign country and that the foreign language must be taught using an appropriate method. Thus he refers to the Somerset course, with which he was closely involved, as being designed 'to develop the receptive skills above all, seeing as its first aim the need for the pupil to grasp what was going on around him, rather than to struggle painfully to produce a minimal number of correct sentences'.

King has spelled this out in more detail. Selecting understanding, speaking and reading as the relevant skills and 'basic ingredients necessary for a language course aimed at *information retrieval*,' he goes on to identify three areas of language needing special attention— pupil questions, enthusing and politeness.

How understanding, reading and speaking can be incorporated into a syllabus is shown in the Somerset course proposals (Appendix A). The inclusion of a modern language component presents many difficulties which stem from what it is hoped to achieve and the suggestions as to suitable methods to employ in classroom teaching.

If doubt is expressed about the appropriateness of the study of modern languages for pupils of average and below average abilities then the whole discussion about teaching method may be rendered irrelevant. Such doubts have been forcibly expressed by Lawton (1973) who concludes that learning a language is 'something which we have to look at very carefully, using a kind of educational cost-benefit analysis. The cost in terms of time spent is hardly worth the benefit achieved. When we are faced with the argument that the timetable is overcrowded we have to look very carefully at such luxuries as modern languages *for the whole school*'. He would not deny children with the aptitude and inclination the opportunity to study a foreign language but he goes on to argue that there are more pressing areas of study for the great majority of pupils. It is cost in terms of time spent about which he is most concerned.

This concern with economy of time may be viewed from two standpoints. Lawton has emphasized the pressure on a pupil's timetable in the few years of his formal schooling. The pressure on the teacher's limited time is also important.

Extending the teaching of modern languages across the ability range has produced an increased demand for qualified language teachers. In the 1960s and early 1970s there has been a shortage of these specialists and for the curriculum planner this has presented a difficult problem: who should be taught by the qualified teachers? Either the qualified teachers should go to the pupils with aptitude, an inclination and an interest in modern languages or to the less-motivated pupils. The argument that language specialists ought not to devote their energies and time to teaching small amounts of language and large amounts of other topics ('background' or 'civilization' studies) is a powerful one.

Without doubt the teaching of European Studies to pupils in the first two years of comprehensive schools has become part of the debate over equality of curricular opportunity. If French is to be taught to one child then, some would argue, it should be taught to all. To make it palatable to the academically weaker pupils, especially when they are taught in mixed ability groups, much time must be spent arousing their interest, motivating them to learn the language, by using non-language studies.

When the third year of secondary education is reached pupils are commonly given a number of courses from which to choose. Able children are steered towards modern language options (sometimes being advised and encouraged to take two modern languages) and for the less able French Studies and European Studies are sometimes offered. These latter courses are terminal courses in that they end when the pupils leave school at the age of sixteen years.

The able children studying French, German or Spanish may well receive a course of European Studies in the sixth form, having already been examined in modern languages at GCE Ordinary or CSE levels. Kilner (1975) has stated bluntly why a language element is not a feature of the sixth form European Studies course which he co-ordinates in a grammar school: 'Some pupils would be studying a language at A level; others might never have studied one at O level; others might never have studied a foreign language. For the first two groups a smattering of French or German was felt to be a waste of valuable course time while for the third group it was felt that the effort and time consumed to learn a basic "First Aid" language at that stage in the school might kill their interest in the rest of the course'.

This dilemma shows no signs of being easily resolved. Neather (1973) has stated that 'European Studies as a whole are too important to leave to the linguists'. Undoubtedly these teachers, who are in short supply, generally lack the expertise to teach those aspects of pan-European society which are the essence of serious European Study (modern language teachers could argue with some justification that many teachers of history and geography are equally ill-equipped). A few teachers have followed new courses of European Studies in universities, colleges and polytechnics, but for the majority their degree courses have provided a non-language competence only in very small geographical areas, usually France or Germany. Hence the obvious preference of some schools for introducing French Studies or German Studies rather than European Studies. The heart of the dilemma whether to include a language element in a European Studies course lies partly in the most efficient use of the pupils' and teachers' time, both of which are in very short supply. It also lies in the aims of European Studies courses. If the four aims outlined in the last chapter—social, cultural, political and vocational—are acceptable as being comprehensive then to which of these does a modern language study contribute? Many European Studies courses originate in teachers being aware of pupils who appear unable to learn French. To argue that pupils can apply linguistic skills to learning within European Studies courses would, on this basis, be an idealistic statement which ignores the reality of teaching. Only for the most able linguists and for those studying European Studies in higher education are the benefits of studying foreign texts and conversing with French or German nationals in their own languages going to be available. Even for these students the language gives access only to restricted regions—French-speaking Europe or German-speaking Europe. This leads to a consideration of how much of Europe one needs to study to make it worthwhile.

What is Europe?
There are two ways of seeking answers to this perplexing problem. On the one hand the search can begin by reviewing data derived from the writings of philosophers, historians, geographers, political scientists, economists, and other experts who have investigated the concept of Europe in an attempt to define its distinctive characteristics. On the other hand data can be obtained from the content of school courses where teachers have defined Europe in their own way often employing traditions and conventions derived from experience within school subjects. There are obviously links between these two approaches though the debate can go on at two different levels without any attempt to establish these links.

Occasionally it is argued that if you cannot define the spatial limits of Europe then you cannot begin to teach European Studies. In defining such limits it would appear, at least to the layman, that the definition of Europe is a problem for the geographer. After all 'Europe is a geographical expression', but as any atlas or regional textbook clearly shows there is no generally accepted geographical definition of Europe. This problem of definition is highlighted by the maps of Europe published in atlases. Frequently the eastern frontier of the continent is marked only by the frame of the map, a vertical line runs from north to south through the middle of the Soviet Union, sometimes to the west of the Urals, sometimes to the east. And deciding how far Turkey is European presents further problems on the eastern frontier. Frequently geographers escape the problem of definition by dispensing with the continent of Europe and employing the concept of Eurasia instead.

Wake (1971) has dismissed the spatial problem as being insoluble and in response to the question 'What is Europe?' chooses to answer in these terms: 'Europe in the long run is a set of ideas and attitudes backed for a long time by technological development far in advance of that of any other area in the world'. He asserts that the cultivation of a sense of Europe, the asking of questions about 'What is Europe?' are 'bound to be the special responsibility of history teachers'. He outlines how this special responsibility might be expressed in the content of courses (Wake 1973) when he proposes that in a thematic syllabus the following cultural areas or influences must be incorporated: (a) the Judaic—and the Islamic; (b) the Graeco-Byzantine, developing into the Slavonic; (c) the Roman-Carolingian; (d) the Scandinavian-Anglo Saxon; (e) the Celtic; (f) the technological revolution that has transformed the world (perhaps the most important).

As for the 'central, unavoidable themes' he proposes: 'nationalism and stereotypes; the centrality of politics; industrialization and urbanization; the spiritual and cultural achievement'.

Here Wake attempts to bridge the two approaches referred to above. At the same time he contributes to an elucidation of the cultural and political aims of European Studies discussed in Chapter 1.

Another interesting attempt at a definition was made by Brugmans (1971) who, in response to the question 'What features and phenomena can be described as European?', replied 'We can quote some examples. We are saying Europe when we talk about Romanesque Art, Gothic Architecture, the Renaissance, Humanism, the Reformation, Classicism, the Baroque era, and the Age of Reason. The list can easily be made longer by mentioning the Romantics, Realism, Trade-unionism —which, it is true, varies so much in the different countries—the Socialist Movement or the Christian Democrats'.

These high priority concepts and topics are a long way from the often ill-assorted collections of facts about regional foods, eating habits, festivals, leisure pursuits, continental journeys, famous buildings and personalities which pass as the central elements in some European Studies courses. Peggotty Freeman was particularly critical of such courses when she described the general picture of European Studies in schools in 1973 as revealing 'confusion, lack of clarity about objectives and over-hasty establishment of courses which tend towards superficiality, reinforcement of stereotyped views about foreigners and a selection of activities which will keep the children quiet'. (Freeman 1973). Part of this confusion has arisen because the transmission of cultural phenomena—whether it be at the simple level of wine and cheese in France or the more difficult level of Romanesque Art—to children in secondary schools must occur either within the framework of traditional school subjects or within a framework of new courses. European Studies courses, as well as French Studies and German Studies courses, are attempts at the latter solution. Some of them incline to the simple, others to the more difficult, from what passes as being more concrete to what passes as being more abstract.

The main point is that if a European Studies course is to lay claim to this label then it must be European in extent and a search must be made by teachers and pupils for phenomena which are distinctly European. If we were to conclude after careful investigation that such phenomena could not be identified in present-day Europe then the case for a course of *contemporary* European Studies would have no validity and an historical approach would be imperative. Since courses of European history already exist in many schools the need for such courses under the title European Studies would cease to exist.

The search for European phenomena worth introducing to pupils attending secondary schools, the second approach referred to at the beginning of this section, has been carried on for many years particularly through the Council for Cultural Co-operation of the Council of Europe. Of the many publications of the CCC, which was set up in 1962, 'Introducing Europe to Senior Pupils' (Jotterand 1966) is probably of most interest to European Studies teachers. It was written to put some flesh on the bones of a resolution adopted by Ministers' Deputies at the Council of Europe on 6 October 1964. Entitled 'Civics and European Education' the first part of this document lists five considerations, one of which reads, 'considering that, at a time when Europe is becoming a reality, it is the imperative duty of secondary education to inculcate into its pupils an awareness of European facts and problems'. Governments, signatory or acceding to the European Cultural Convention, were encouraged to draw up a European Civics syllabus which 'can serve as a model for possible school curricula' and 'do everything within their power to ensure that all disciplines concerned—for instance history, geography, literature, modern languages—contribute to the creation of a European consciousness' (Jotterand 1966). For an up-dated statement on the same lines see the Janne Report published by the Commission of the European Communities in 1973.

For teachers of upper forms in secondary schools it was suggested that these ten lessons could be given as a step towards inculcating an awareness of European facts and problems:

Lesson 1 The European Idea through the Centuries.
Lesson 2 From Victor Hugo to Winston Churchill.
Lesson 3 What is Europe?
Lesson 4 Towards a United Europe: three conceptions of union, obstacles, grounds for hope.
Lesson 5 The Council of Europe.
Lesson 6 The European Communities.
Lessons 7 and 8   Some aspects of European Co-operation.
Lesson 9 Europe between the Great Powers.
Lesson 10 Europe and the World.

As has already been mentioned in Chapter 1, in the post-war decades the movement towards social, political, economic and cultural integration in western Europe has prompted institutions like the European Communities, NATO and the Council of Europe to encourage schoolteachers in the member states to include European topics in their syllabuses. The 'idea of Europe' underlying this belongs to the future and is based on a belief that step by step generations to come will witness the emergence of a new conception of European citizenship which will supplement or even replace national citizenship for the residents of a spatially defined 'new Europe'. Some see a tension between suggestions that the emphasis should be upon the future and suggestions that the emphasis should be upon the cultural heritage of Europe. Both of these notions are contrary to arguments that where Europeans are gathered together in any numbers there *is* Europe. Arguments stemming from this point of view extend the spatial area of study far beyond the continental limits familiar from school atlases to a world study in which European influences to be emphasized are carefully selected.

Few teachers appear to be inclined to analyse critically the question 'What is Europe?' whether it be from geographical, historical, futuristic or broadly cultural points of view. This would seem to be outside their sphere, to be an activity appropriate for academics in higher education. A preferred starting point is 'what aspects of the everyday lives of Europeans can I talk about to my pupils?' In emphasizing the *typical* activities of Frenchmen or Germans, Poles or Danes as they go about their daily work, travelling from place to place, eating *typical* foods using *typical* eating habits in *typical* houses in *typical* streets in *typical* towns or villages, teachers can be accused of superficiality, stereotyping and simplistic pedestrianism. Undoubtedly, there are some courses in some schools which warrant such criticisms. The principles on which they are grounded may be valid, for example, in some courses where the over-riding principle may be starting from the known (the child's experience of everyday life in his home area in Britain) and then moving to the unknown which provides a basis for exercises in making comparisons and contrasts, and also in developing empathy between the pupils and selected foreigners.

Another principle is that pupils can understand simple human relationships, as in basic family relationships, which can be placed in distant environmental and institutional settings, thus extending the child's understanding of more and more foreign situations. Whatever the reasoning and rationalizing courses which produce little more than assemblages of ill-assorted and badly stereotyped data must be improved to become more worthwhile areas of endeavour for pupils in school. Appendix A includes examples of course outlines from Oxfordshire and Somerset and course syllabuses from two schools plus a syllabus published by a GCE examination board. These indicate the definitions of Europe currently employed in schools and provide guidance for teachers new to the field of European Studies to what some of their colleagues consider to be worthwhile topics for study.

CHAPTER THREE

Course Organization

Having reviewed the aims and objectives of European Studies courses and considered in the previous chapter two of the most difficult problems in defining the substantive area of such courses, the place of a modern language and the limits of 'Europe', we can move to the ways in which courses are organized in secondary schools. Although the history of European Studies courses is short, there is, as with many curricular innovations, no evidence of stability within individual courses in particular schools or in geographical areas. Experimentation continues with schools adding new topics, preparing new resource materials, adding or rejecting large components such as a modern language, devising new teaching arrangements and timetables and devising new forms of pupil assessment. Evidence of these changes can be found in comparing school syllabuses in European Studies over a period of time or examining the products of working parties of teachers. A good example of this is provided in the Somerset proposals, the original draft of which is included in Appendix A. This has already been replaced by a new, revised draft and, no doubt, this will in time be replaced by another version. In this chapter the focus is upon course organization and particularly with the relationship between the organization of subject matter and of teachers to cover it.

European Studies are interdisciplinary, pupil-centred and enquiry-based. These three catch-words of contemporary curricular jargon place European Studies firmly in the 'romantic' sector (see Chapter 1) of education. It is these three concepts which seem to recur in the courses in Appendix A.

Inter-disciplinary Courses
The very existence of courses labelled European Studies reflects the dissatisfaction felt by some teachers with traditional school subjects. Establishing a new integrated course is seen to be the way of filling a gap in the education of the adolescent. Of course, some inter-disciplinary courses have a long pedigree. One of the earliest and

25

most persuasive arguments for putting geography and history together was proposed as long ago as 1913 by Halford Mackinder, an influential pioneer of the study of geography in secondary and higher education. We can trace the debate over separate subjects and inter-disciplinary courses throughout the 1930s when the Association for Education in Citizenship was specially active to the post-World War II Social Studies Movement (Lawton and Dufour 1973, Williams 1976). Possibly the most important recent injection of new ideas came with the setting up of the Nuffield-Schools Council Humanities Curriculum Project in 1967. The remit given to this project read, 'To offer schools and teachers such stimulus, support and materials as may be appropriate to the mounting, as an element in general education, of enquiry-based courses, which cross the subject boundaries between English, history, geography, religious studies and social studies' (Stenhouse 1969). European Studies courses were already in existence in a few schools when this project started work but many recently formulated courses owe much to the pioneering efforts of the participating teachers and the project team associated with the HCP. This is particularly noticeable in the treatment of controversial issues in European Studies classrooms and in the way resource material is collected, collated and presented to the pupils for study and discussion.

In a more recent publication of the Schools Council, Working Paper 53 (Schools Council 1975b) the authors distinguish three different forms of interdisciplinary courses: first, interdisciplinary studies where teachers continue to work as subject specialists but 'plan their courses in such a way that their treatment of themes of common interest is co-ordinated'; second, core studies where 'a core study is an integrated element within a framework of specialist subjects and has status of a "subject" in its own right', and, third, full integration where all the allocated periods are given over to the study of unified themes. An examination of European Studies courses suggests that all three forms exist for European Studies in British secondary schools.

In the courses quoted in Appendix A the essence of the subject arrangement is an integration of knowledge and skills derived from traditional school subjects and other sources. There is scope, within these courses as in most European Studies courses, for single teachers to be responsible for all the teaching of a course or for groups of teachers to work together in informal or highly-structured team arrangements. In an attempt to classify types of course arrangements appropriate for European Studies James (1973) has identified seven models:

Model 1 Language An arrangement in which a European language is the focal point of the course and provides access to *all* aspects of the life of the linguistic community or country.

Model 2 Service Courses A social science discipline is the centre of this arrangement; cognate disciplines plus a modern language contribute to the study.

Model 3 Area Studies Topic-based courses in which the topics are selected from a linguistic community and language studies are included.

Model 4 Core/Context Model A major subject is studied within courses of European literature/history/thought or European economics/sociology/geography/government. Language study is included.

Model 5 Umbrella Model A combination of several linguistic community (i.e. area) studies, e.g. French Studies plus German Studies.

Model 6 Cold War Model A combination of West European and East European Studies.

Model 7 Common Market Model An area study focusing on the EEC member countries.

These models are based on courses running in universities and polytechnics and similar patterns can be detected in schools. For discussion of European Studies course arrangements in tertiary education see Counter (1974) and Shennan (1974). Thus Model 3 underpins French Studies and German Studies courses and an extension of these courses can be found under the label European Studies when the geographical area studied in the course is that of the EEC (Model 7). If European Studies are to be comprehensive continent-wide studies then Model 6 is the one of most interest for teachers.

The actual model adopted in any school, once the need for European Studies has been accepted, will be determined principally by the staff available. A single enthusiast may plan a course, persuade colleagues to help him to teach it and then submit it for consideration to the working parties, committees or senior staff responsible for curriculum policy in a school. At this level of grass-roots reform the inter-relationship of the participant teachers is a crucial consideration. An original course proposal is likely to be amended by discussion and the nature of the discussion will determine the quality and quantity of the amendments. The actual contribution to the discussion made by any individual will be determined by the power he has and the way he chooses to use it. While there are some European Studies courses which are the brainchild of a teacher who accepts full responsibility for teaching a course single-handed most courses involve more than one teacher. The word 'involve' is used here to mean that the teachers concerned have European Studies as part of their timetable. This requires emphasis since it is clearly possible in a school for a teacher to be involved in a course without being engaged directly in the classroom teaching of the pupils following the course.

Teachers may contribute to European Studies courses in several ways, including: making curriculum resources and equipment available for teacher use; accompanying pupils on study visits; acting as an expert consultant for pupils engaged in special studies or the preparation of projects; contributing occasional special lectures. Such informal but important activities enrich a course, making up for some of the inadequacies of the individual teacher and introducing variety in teaching materials and methods to the pupils. They lead to a more efficient utilization of the total expertise available in a school staff room.

For the teachers the key question in an interdisciplinary course is whether they are to be considered as specialists or generalists. If they are considered specialists then they will contribute to the course content and modes of study derived from their special subject; if they are not then they will be expected to cope with all aspects of the course. Deciding on the appropriate staff arrangement in these terms is one of the most difficult problems encountered in the organization of European Studies courses.

Studies in the theory of curricular integration offer little direct guidance to the teachers in a particular school; they do however provide a rationale for the various alternative structures which could be introduced. The individual school will need to assess critically its overall staffing pattern and its organization. Different solutions to similar problems will be produced according to whether a school has a faculty system in which several departments are co-ordinated by a faculty head or a more conventional subject department system. The arrangement of subjects and courses within departments and faculties is also important. How faculties and departments relate to each other in terms of the overall curriculum policy of a school is another consideration.

Since European Studies courses are frequently taught by teachers of modern languages together with teachers of geography, history and other subjects, then at least two departments and/or two faculties are likely to be involved. Obviously providing a course as a third or a fourth year option is far more complicated than providing a minority-time general studies course in the sixth form. In the latter case there is usually less teaching time involved and often a single teacher can cope with the course; in the former case external examinations are likely to be involved and, in large schools, a European Studies course will need to be slotted into groups of subjects from which pupils will select their options. The working out of a balance between subjects and courses in the total curricular provision for an age or ability group in a particular school requires great care. European Studies as an interdisciplinary course may have to be considered alongside such alternative courses as environmental studies, humanities, integrated science and other area studies such as American Studies or Asian Studies. Deciding whether a pupil who follows a course of European Studies should be excluded from the study of history or geography or a modern language in a particular year is another problem. This is especially serious where external examinations are involved since the decision to take European Studies may give the pupil the chance to acquire only a single examination pass at the end of the course and this is likely to have less currency in a competitive job market then two or more passes in subjects which had to be rejected by the pupil so that he could study European Studies. It is interesting to notice in the revised Somerset proposals (Appendix A) that there are two alternative syllabuses and Syllabus B is described as a 'double-award scheme' which is 'intended to be timetabled as a two-subject course leading to CSE with a full range of grades over two years'.

Team Teaching

Closely associated with interdisciplinary course arrangements are team teaching schemes. Theoretical discussions of team teaching focus on the inter-teacher relationships within teams and the classroom strategies employed to make effective use of them. Anderson (1966) has outlined a team teaching arrangement in which there is a pyramid of staff: at the top is the master teacher responsible for planning and teaching key lessons. He is supported by several teachers who follow up the key lessons with exercises and tutorial help. At the base are the technicians, clerks and auxiliaries who provide technical support including the typing of work sheets and the provision of audio-visual services and library materials.

For those European Studies courses with a modern language component a team teaching arrangement in which a linguist and a non-linguist, or several non-linguists, work together is essential. In some courses the modern language component is taught with little reference to what is going on in the other parts of the course. Thus a sequential structure of course content is devised by the linguist who seeks to develop the language skills—whether they be oral, aural or verbal—of the pupils. Another teacher copes with the non-language elements in which topics may follow one another in succession without any apparent logical sequence. The relationship between teachers in such an arrangement is likely to be very informal, rushed conversations in the teachers' common room around the beginning and end of term often being the principal forms of contact.

Where more than two teachers are working on a European Studies course without languages the team arrangement is likely to be more formal. In some schools a teacher has been designated European Studies Courses Convenor and this teacher has overall responsibility for the course. Included in this are such matters as room timetabling, purchase and hire of teaching materials, organization of study visits, preparing examination papers, liaison with examination boards, organizing formal meetings for the European Studies teachers and co-ordinating courses within a year group or between year groups. In large comprehensive schools where several European Studies courses may be running in any school year the need for a convenor with these responsibilities is evident. While two of his main tasks will be reminding colleagues in other subjects of the existence of the courses and putting pressure on those who control the school's purse strings, keeping the team of European Studies teachers in sufficiently close contact so that their courses retain coherence and purposefulness will be vitally important.

Very few schools have appointed full-time teachers of European Studies: most teachers have a principal commitment to a traditional subject and to this European Studies may be added.

It would be foolish to underestimate the difficulties inherent in establishing a team of teachers working together to teach a single course. Evidence of the difficulties is available from Schools Council projects (e.g. Shipman 1974). Difficulties arise not only in the substantive area of deciding the appropriate content and methods of teaching but also at the personal level. Possibly the most serious difficulty stems from the mobility of teachers. A teaching team requires time and practice to establish efficient modes of communication between the participant teachers and to develop sound teaching strategies. In this respect a teaching team may be compared with a team of footballers. Any change in the membership of the team is likely to slow down the team's progress. It may well be that teachers who are attracted to innovations are by definition ambitious and mobile. It is striking that of the convenors of the first four CSE Mode 3 European Studies courses approved by one board, one became an HMI, another a local inspector, and the other two deputy headteachers, within four years of initiating their courses.

The essence of a team teaching arrangement is the efficient use of the expertise available in a group of teachers. This expertise may be in the fields of content, teaching method, resource collection or pupil evaluation.

Key lessons, given by a single teacher to a large group composed of several classes, have been experimented with in some schools. Such lessons are attended by members of the teaching team who follow up the key lessons in other lessons with their own classes. Sometimes the teacher who gives the key lesson prepares worksheets linked to his lesson and other teachers supervise the completion of these, offering personal help to individual pupils when the need arises and marking all the sheets for their own classes. Classes may also combine to watch a film or a television broadcast, or to listen to a tape-recording, a radio broadcast or a guest speaker.

From this it will be appreciated that team teaching is an important part of resource management: for schools with little money available for resource collection and storage the expertise of the teaching staff will be *the* major resource. How staff and whatever other resources available to a school will be utilised in the classroom will be determined by the teaching modes favoured by the teachers involved in the course. These teaching modes and the ways in which pupils learn European Studies are the concern of the second part of this book.

Part II

Learning and Teaching

CHAPTER FOUR

Aspects of Learning European Studies

Earlier it was stated that European Studies courses are child-centred and enquiry-based. An educationist who has provided a lucid rationale for such approaches is Torsten Husen. He writes, 'much of that which occurs in the process we call teaching rests upon two premises, which are usually not made explicit. The first is that the pupil learns something not because it is attractive or pleasing, but to avoid disagreeable consequences if he does not learn it. . . . The second premise is that the teacher is the *primus motor* who keeps the pupils going. He hands over the lessons and makes sure his pupils do them. No essential spontaneous learning activity on the pupil's part is assumed. He is often conceived as the willing recipient of the knowledge that the teacher transmits to him' (1974).

This caricature of the 'drinking-glass model' is changing as teachers are affected by changes in society, advances in technology and the expansion of knowledge. As Husen explains, 'these days the teacher is not so much a fountainhead of knowledge as a man who taps its sources and guides his pupils to them. It is he who mobilizes the information, the material to be learned'. Hence the 'teacher must give more of himself to the organization of learning opportunities for the individual pupil . . . the instructional ideal is total individualization'.

To explain this emphasis upon the individual and the swing away from teacher-centred instruction to pupil-centred learning requires an analysis of psychological, sociological and social psychological theories and research findings. There is no simple explanation and yet the products of this change are plainly evident—though in some schools more than others. Staffing structure, timetables, class organization, examination procedures, all reflect the trend which is encompassed in the umbrella term 'curriculum innovation'. For the practising teacher any innovation becomes significant when it implies changes in *his* classroom. The introduction of new course content does not necessarily imply any change in teaching method. European Studies courses are at first an innovation in which the emphasis is upon a particular content.

35

Since the content is derived partly from traditional school subjects and is taught by teachers trained through and experienced in traditional subjects we ought to expect that the teaching methods employed in European Studies classes will be an amalgam of strategies from several subjects.

The success of a European Studies course, like any other school course, must be judged in terms of what the pupils have learned. Curriculum theorists have utilized the findings of psychologists, especially Bruner, Piaget and Gagné to define developmental stages in the intellectual growth of a child and to classify learning activities into hierarchical structures. It is to be expected that sensitive teachers aware of the developmental stages which their pupils have reached will seek to

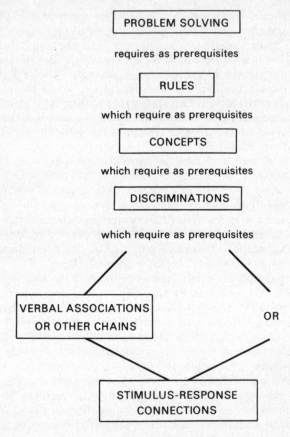

Fig. 1

develop teaching strategies and techniques which will take their pupils to higher levels of learning activity.

Gagné places problem-solving at the top of his ladder of intellectual skills and demonstrates that to acquire this level of intellectual activity a pupil must already have acquired an array of other learning activities. He presents this ladder diagrammatically as in Fig. 1 (Gagné 1970).

Before applying this ladder to the teaching of European Studies it is worth noting the phases which Gagné has elaborated in an act of learning:

Motivation Phase   Time
EXPECTANCY
    Apprehending Phase
    ATTENTION
    SELECTIVE PERCEPTION
       Acquisition Phase
       CODING
       STORAGE ENTRY
          Retention Phase
          MEMORY
          STORAGE
             Recall Phase
             RETRIEVAL
                Generalization Phase
                TRANSFER
                   Performance Phase
                   RESPONDING
                      Feedback Phase
                      REINFORCEMENT

Fig. 2. The phases of an act of learning and associated processes (Gagné 1974)

For the teacher, then, the task is to elaborate strategies and techniques of teaching which will facilitate pupils' learning as indicated in the sequence in Fig 2, and also proceed to higher levels of intellectual activity, as in Fig. 1.

In Chapter 1, we noted that objectives are of three kinds—cognitive, affective and behavioural skills. By looking more closely at problem-solving, concept-formation and attitude-change, we can associate the delineation of aims and objectives with learning-development and then go on to consider teaching methods.

Problem-Solving

Gagné has outlined the sequence of events involved in problem-solving. 'The initial event is the *presentation of the problem*, which may be done by means of a verbal statement or otherwise. The learner then *defines the problem*, that is, he distinguishes the essential features of the situation. As a third step he *formulates hypotheses* which may be applicable to a solution. Finally, he carries out *verification* of his hypothesis or of successive ones, until he finds one that achieves the solution he seeks' (Gagné 1970).

In a classroom the teacher is responsible for a clear presentation of a worthwhile problem. From then on the pupil, under guidance and having *already* acquired relevant rules and concepts, sets about solving the problem. The process of problem-solving is described by some as discovery-learning and it is important to stress that while the process of problem-solving is in itself significant in the pupil's education what is learned at the end, i.e. what has been discovered, is also significant. The argument that knowing facts is less important than knowing how to obtain facts is one which is dangerous for its half-truths.

Teachers engage in promoting problem-solving when they devise hypothesis-testing exercises, educational games, role-playing activities and simulations, projects and when they set examination questions or homework assignments in which pupils are presented with problems to solve. In study visits, at home or overseas, problem-solving of a very practical kind is likely to be a feature. Problem-solving is the terminal activity in a sequence of phases and its success as a teaching strategy will be determined largely by the attention given by the teacher in ensuring that the earlier phases have been thoroughly covered. Not only is it necessary for the pupils to have acquired concepts and rules also they must be proficient, *through practice*, in the study skills needed to acquire new concepts and rules and in their utilization for solving novel problems.

Concept-Formation

Discussion of concept-formation is hampered not only by the fundamental problem of defining what precisely a concept is but also by the confusion that arises when one moves from the psychological research literature containing innumerable laboratory experiments that deal with the strategies employed by individuals in forming concepts, to the educational literature which emphasizes teacher-class or teacher-pupil interactions which lead to concept-formation. Carroll (1964) has emphasized 'The teaching of words, and of the meanings and concepts they designate or convey, is one of the principal tasks of teachers at all levels of education', and goes on to define concepts as 'the abstracted and often cognitively structured classes of "mental" experience learned by organisms in the course of their life histories'. In order to form a concept a pupil must notice that a particular new experience has some feature(s) in common with other experiences he has had and then by a process of abstraction and classification concepts are formed. What matters is that the learner shall himself see which of the features of the new experience are significant.

Carroll has sought to clarify this process by citing illustrations of concept teaching problems. One which is of special interest to teachers of European Studies is discussed by Carroll under the heading 'Tourist versus Immigrant'.

'If the child is presented with various instances of people who are either tourists or immigrants, properly labelled as such, but with no further explanation, it will be the child's task to figure out what attributes or characteristics are relevant to the differentiation of these concepts. They might occur either in school or outside of school. Most likely the instances of tourists and immigrants will be relatively sporadic over time and the instances may not vary in such a way as to show what attributes are truly relevant. . . . If the natural environment is like a grand concept-formation experiment, it may take the child a long time to attain the concepts *tourist* and *immigrant*; indeed the environment may not be as informative as the usual experimenter, since the child may not always be informed, or reliably informed, as to the correctness of his guesses. . . . The purpose of teaching is to short-cut the capricious process of concept attainment within the natural environment. Through the use of language, there should be relatively little difficulty in explaining to a child that an immigrant is one who moves from one country or region to another in order to change his permanent residence, while a tourist is one who travels around for pleasure without changing his permanent residence. One can use simple explanations like "He's going to stay here, have his home here . . ." or "He's just travelling around for the fun of it while he's on vacation, and some day he'll get back home". There should be no difficulty, at any rate, if the child has already mastered certain prerequisite concepts. Among these prerequisite concepts would be: the concept of home or permanent residence and all that it implies; the concept of the division of world territory into different countries and those in turn into regions; and the concept of travelling for pleasure or curiosity. It is very likely that the child who is having trouble understanding the concept of tourist *v.* the concept of immigrant has not got clearly in mind the prerequisite notions that constitute, in fact, the criterial attributes upon which the distinction hangs.'

Acknowledging that concepts can be taught leads to a basic distinction between procedures adopted in their teaching. This is the distinction between inductive and deductive procedures. In the former the pupil is presented by the teacher with a number of positive and negative instances of a concept and the pupil must infer the nature of the concept by selecting the criterial attributes. In the deductive procedure concepts are presented to the pupils through verbal definition or description. This latter procedure is a short-cut device by which the pupil is freed from exploring numerous examples.

In an unpublished dissertation Knowles (1972) has explored the place of concepts in a European Studies course. After referring to the writings of Sigel, Gagné, de Cecco and Crabtree she proceeds to Taba's classification of concepts into three levels: key, main and organizing. For a course of European Studies Knowles designates three groups, or clusters, of key concepts: (a) diversity, interdependence, co-operation; (b) power, causality, social control; (c) tradition, cultural change, values. Taking each of these in turn she identifies main and organizing concepts associated with each one.

(a)

Key	*Diversity* that diversity is the chief characteristic of contemporary European society
Main	that this diversity is often misrepresented as national stereotypes
Organizing	that an understanding of the origins of national characteristics will reduce the risk of stereotyping and increase the appreciation of individual characteristics
Key	*Interdependence* that persons and groups depend upon other persons and groups for satisfaction of needs
Main	behaviour of each person and group affects other persons and groups
Organizing	acceptance of interdependence indicates mature level of development and leads to a sympathy and desire for communication and co-operation
Key	*Co-operation* the solution of important human problems requires human beings to engage in joint effort
Main	the more complex society is, the more co-operation is required
Organizing	co-operation often requires compromise and postponement of immediate satisfactions—in this way it is possible to resolve differences in the attempt to find solutions

(b)

Key	*Power*
	the amount of influence which groups and individuals have in making decisions which affect other people varies
Main	the extent of this influence depends on social and political organization
Organizing	the desire for power often leads to conflict though sometimes it can lead to a demand for closer co-operation
Key	*Causality*
	events can often be made meaningful by studying their antecedents
Main	events usually result from a number of antecedents coming together in a certain unit of space and time
Organizing	it may no longer be true in view of the exponential rate of change that studying past events helps us either to understand the future or interpret the present
Key	*Societal Control*
	all societies influence and attempt to mould the conduct of their members by precept, example, reward or punishment
Main	there is a great variety in the way these are operated within different societies resulting in a wide variation in the amount of personal freedom
Organizing	everyone belongs to many groups with overlapping membership and often conflicting demands on members: church, family, school, state. Each by exerting controls shapes the personality structure and behaviour of its members

(c)

Key	*Tradition*
	societies and groups and individuals within them tend to retain many traditional values, attitudes and ways of living
Main	sometimes these are inappropriate in dealing with current problems
Organizing	certain institutions in society, such as the family, religion and education tend to change less rapidly than do other elements of societies

Key   *Cultural Change*
           culture never remains static though the context of the
           change (economic, political, sociological and techno-
           logical), the speed of change, and the importance of the
           change vary greatly

Main   cultural change is accelerated by such factors as
           increased knowledge, mobility, and communication
           both within and between cultures

Organizing cultural values which are transmitted by the mass
           media and increased mobility of population are tending
           towards a decultivated norm

Key   *Values*
           those objects, behaviour, ideas, or institutions which a
           society or an individual considers important and
           desires, constitute values

Main   societies and individuals often differ significantly in the
           values they hold

Organizing that in spite of unifying influences of industrialization,
           urbanization and growth of mass media, the values of
           Europe remain as diverse as ever

The identification of key, main and organizing concepts is a
constructive exercise for teachers in the planning of their courses, the
concepts provide a guide to the selection of appropriate teaching
techniques and the associated resource materials.

Attitude-Change
'To seek to increase international goodwill with special reference to
European societies.' 'To create an awareness of the similarities and
differences between European countries, so as to develop
understanding and tolerance.'

In the lists of aims and objectives quoted in Chapter 1 these
statements are to be found together with others which, less frankly,
seek the same ends. If European Studies courses are about anything at
all they are about international understanding. Teachers, when
discussing European Studies courses, will sometimes imply that their
pupils are unfavourably prejudiced towards foreigners in general or
individual nations and their citizens in particular and will stress the
hope that in teaching European Studies they will alter these
prejudices—'for the better'!

Flying in the face of the old adage 'familiarity breeds contempt' there
is a clear assumption in much European Studies teaching that more
and more knowledge about European nations produces favourable

attitudes to those nations. This assumption is supported by empirical evidence. Much the most detailed examination of international attitudes is to be found in Kelman's collection of studies (1965). A particularly relevant contribution is Scott's (1965) where, after reviewing a number of research studies, the author concludes 'benign images of the world and a desire for co-operative involvement in it will more frequently be found among the well-informed segments of the population than among the poorly informed'.

However the accumulation of knowledge is not the only source of attitude-formation. Morrison and McIntyre (1971) suggest four others.

(a) *Identification.* Children form emotional attachments to other persons and from these attachments they generalize their feelings to institutions, such as a nation, e.g. liking or disliking a foreign political figure, sportsman or musician is generalized to that person's nation and they may imitate the other person's life style, ideas, dress or mannerisms without any direct teaching occurring.

(b) *Cognitive development.* Children and adolescents are assumed to be interested in the world around them and in interpreting the phenemona they observe (Adelson and O'Neill 1966). This results in 'major advances in their capacities for acquiring and handling concepts, and for sophisticated appraisal and solution of problems' (Morrison and McIntyre 1971).

This aspect of attitude-formation is of direct relevance to the European Studies teacher. To explain it more carefully a theoretical analysis by Scott is helpful. He writes, 'If Russia is seen in terms of its size, climate, geography, location, scientific accomplishments and military power, this particular image implies that these concepts exist in the mind of the viewer as attributes that can potentially be applied to all nations. The attributes conceived by an individual as applying to nation-objects may be represented as a set of lines in multi-dimensional space, and the nation-images to which they are applied may be regarded as intersections of the lines' (Scott 1965). (See Fig. 3.)

As the European Studies teacher seeks to develop an image of a particular area, whether it be a small town, a region, a nation, a group of nations, or the whole European continent, he will select data for the pupil to assimilate. Each separate piece of information is an attribute, which, when combined with other attributes, leads to the creation of images. He may select *only* favourable attributes, quite unintentionally. He may also encourage his pupils to transfer attributes appropriate to one area to another area. The selection of information and the way in which it is presented to and organized for the pupils is clearly of considerable importance. An example of the way this could work out in a classroom is for a teacher to present a case study of a small peasant farm in southern Italy, selecting such features (attributes) as size, crops,

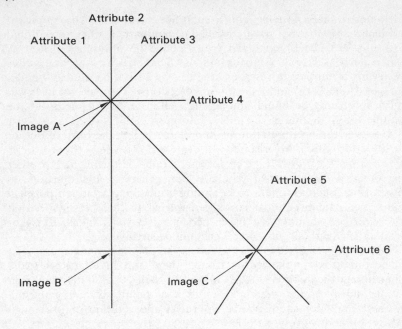

Fig. 3. The relationship between images and attributes (Scott 1965)

production and marketing methods, and then generalizing from the study to describe it as 'Mediterranean farming'. Similarly, a study of the national political system of East Germany might be used to make generalizations about East European governments. Not all attributes appropriate to one image may be transferable to other images. If teachers purposefully select only those attributes which will create either favourable or unfavourable attitudes, and intentionally conceal or under-represent other attitudes then they may justifiably be accused of engaging in propaganda in classrooms.

European Studies teachers, like teachers of current affairs, politics, moral education, religious education and history, need to be alert to the possibility that they are engaged in indoctrination and/or propaganda.

(c) *Psychodynamics.* In this context attitudes towards foreigners and foreign nations may arise from the personality system of the individual. Scott comments '. . . there is substantive evidence of a widespread disposition either to like or dislike foreign countries in general, that is, a favourable attitude to one country is associated with a favourable attitude to all others' (1965). Research by psychologists into extremism, whether of ideology or political action, has attempted to relate extremism to such personality traits as aggressiveness. An example of this is provided by Eysenck's study of the political ideologies held by adults (1954). He defined two dimensions of attitudes, one he termed radicalism-conservatism and the other toughmindedness-tendermindedness. By drawing these as two intersecting axes it was possible to position an individual in regard to political attitudes and personality characteristics.

(d) *Normative.* This is the last of the four groups in Morrison and McIntyre's classification. They write 'individuals acquire the attitudes that are appropriate to their culture, social class and group backgrounds, and the role expectations that others hold for them'. For the teacher of European Studies this has two important implications. First, if certain attitudes are the products of social pressures how far can the teacher in a school setting hope to modify such attitudes? Can his pressure counter the prevailing pressures built up over time in the environment outside the school? Second, is it possible in this context to define 'right' and 'wrong' attitudes? The empirical evidence coming from the burgeoning field of political socialization is not particularly encouraging for the teacher wishing to convert anti-European or anti-German, anti-French or generally xenophobic pupils to more favourable attitudes.

An interesting study was conducted by Mercer in which he investigated political learning according to the age of school pupils in Scotland. In particular he sought to assess the contribution of Modern Studies to the political learning of those pupils who took this course. Modern Studies is examined at Ordinary grade and Higher grade of the Scottish Certificate of Education and generally it is studied by pupils of average and below average ability in the upper parts of secondary schools (Williams 1969). The syllabuses contain sizeable European elements. Mercer concludes from his studies that 'too much is expected of formal political education in too short a time and at too late a stage in the adolescent's political development. Modern Studies has been established with too grandiose expectations which ignore or downgrade the possibility that factors outside the school, as well as other factors in the school environment beside the curriculum, will not only be a major source of influence in political learning long before children are eligible to take Modern Studies, but operate while they are still taking the course, and will continue long after the school has been left well behind. To saddle a school course with the heavy responsibility for stimulating political attitudes when outside pressures have already instilled in the child a contrary impression of the world is seen to be in blatant disregard for the main features of political learning'. Mercer contends that the influence of the schools, expressed in a few hours of weekly instruction, cannot counter the overwhelming influences outside the curriculum.

So far there has been no published empirical research into the impact of European Studies courses upon adolescents and thus it is impossible to assess whether the attitudes of pupils who follow such courses are fundamentally different from those who have not followed the courses. Given the impact of the mass media plus the more direct personal socializing influences of parents and peers we ought not to be surprised or disappointed if teaching European Studies produces little change in pupils' attitudes.

CHAPTER FIVE

Teaching Techniques

In an ideal world a teacher of European Studies would have access to
abundant reference books, an efficient storage and retrieval system for
up-to-date reference materials including articles, photographs and
statistical data, a store of slides, filmstrips, film loops and films;
recording and transmitting facilities for radio and colour television
broadcasts; articulate experts available with firsthand knowledge and
experience of topics to be studied; facilities for study visits abroad
without cost to the pupils; opportunities for independent study visits for
the teacher; keen pupils; supportive parents; co-operative colleagues;
an enthusiastic headteacher; a sympathetic and affluent local
education authority. Most importantly he would have the *time* to
produce improved resource materials, examine alternative teaching
strategies and techniques, engage in purposeful discussions with
colleagues, tutor individuals or groups of pupils and plan courses in
detail. In a real world teachers have to settle for far less. It is not
uncommon to encounter teachers who run European Studies courses
without any budgetary resources in unsuitable classrooms utilizing
textbooks purchased for other courses and entirely dependent on 'chalk
and talk' as their sole teaching methodology. Good teachers may well
succeed in such situations though not without a great deal of
frustration and complaint.

The principal teaching problem for the European Studies teacher is
devising teaching strategies which will effectively bring Europe into the
classroom. A study visit to another European country is the most
obvious way of achieving this goal. While this may sound illogical—to
bring Europe into the classroom you must take your pupils to Europe—
it highlights the need: (a) to provide primary, first hand, experiences for
pupils; (b) to support study visits by thorough preparation and
follow-up activities in the classroom; (c) to know one part of mainland
Europe well to serve as a basis for comparisons and contrasts; (d) to
seek alternatives to study visits should such visits prove impossible for
whole classes or individuals in a class.

47

The Organization of Study Visits

The connection between study visits to mainland Europe and courses in European Studies is fundamental. The local education authorities in which European Studies courses are most numerous are those which have established an array of exchanges, links and study visits. Oxfordshire, Somerset, Leicestershire and Hertfordshire are areas which are in the forefront. The scope and variety of British educational links with mainland Europe can be gauged by reading publications of the Central Bureau for Educational Visits and Exchanges, in particular the journal, *Educational Exchange*, which is published three times a year.

It is possible to consider educational links between a British school and selected parts of Europe as part of a continuum in which one end of the continuum would be represented by the school-organized foreign holiday and the other end would be a study visit which formed an integral part of a specific course of study. In between these two limits can be placed the array of contacts which includes person-to-person exchanges, home-to-home exchanges, school class-to-school class exchanges, sports exchanges, joint cultural and sporting activities, and joint holidays and cruises.

The crucial consideration for the teacher of a European Studies course is whether a study visit is a means or an end. If the study visit is viewed as an end then the subject matter of classroom studies will focus sharply upon the area to be visited. The European Studies course may well be developed as an area study in this regard and topics studied will be confined to those directly relevant to the study area. If the essential ingredient of the study visit is living in a foreign *milieu* as the foreigners live then social elements are likely to figure strongly in the course. However, if a study visit is seen as a means then the area to be visited is likely to be selected on quite different criteria. Exploration visits or visits designed to enable pupils to experiment with particular study techniques, e.g. surveying by using triangulation in a mountainous area or measuring the movement of glacial ice. The fact that the subject of study happens to be in a foreign country is simply a complication and thus the 'European Study' must be undertaken in order to ensure the efficient administration of the study. Generally study visits of the 'end' variety are associated with school-based European Studies.

Given the rich tradition of home-based study visits which geographers have inherited and developed it is the geographer who is likely to make the most positive contribution to the organization of study visits for European Studies pupils. The geographer should be able to select an appropriate study area once the criteria for selecting an area have been defined. Ideally, teachers should be given time and financial backing to make a thorough reconnaissance of a potential study area. The geographer should be able to obtain relevant maps and guide pupils in interpreting basic data on foreign maps. He should be able to specify worthwhile tasks for pupils to undertake including accurate observation and description, collection of data and its application to prove hypotheses or contribute to the solution of carefully defined problems. The sort of problems to be studied will, of course, be determined by the aims contained in the European Studies syllabus and by whether the study visit is an integral part of the course or a peripheral extra. Whatever topics are studied on a foreign visit care must be taken to ensure that they could not be just as easily studied in a British classroom.

What can be accomplished by a group of thirty sixth-formers and their teachers on a study visit to Yugoslavia has been outlined by Kilner. Examples of their studies include the effects of tourism on small communities in southern Dalmatia; the contrast between the traditional way of life in the Popove Polje, some twenty miles inland, with developments in the area of the Bay of Zupa; and the commercialized forms of agriculture in the Neretva Delta. That these studies could be accomplished in a part of Yugoslavia in which the pupils would be unlikely to have anything more than a few words in the local language shows that non-language based European Studies courses can be of great value.

The teacher contemplating his first foreign study visit should read the Schools Council's publication, *Out and About* (Schools Council 1972a). Here detailed advice is given concerning the organization of school groups and if this advice is taken seriously many of the pitfalls encountered by inexperienced teachers should be avoided. There is general agreement that the success of a visit is proportionate to the amount of attention paid to detailed planning. For the European Studies teacher planning and administrative problems need to be as few as possible since they can only impair the progress of the pupils in attaining their study objectives.

The material end-products of European Studies visits are likely to take the same form as those from home-based study visits. They include sketch-maps, diagrams, field-sketches, photographs, colour transparencies, scrapbooks, tape recordings and 8mm ciné films. An increasingly popular feature of British geographical field courses is the inclusion of data-recording exercises which supplement the more traditional activities focusing upon accurate observation and recording. Pupils are grouped and presented with a problem to solve or a hypothesis to verify. Questionnaires may be prepared and these may be the basis for recorded interviews with samples of the local population. Clearly, exercises of this kind are only possible if pupils can converse with the interviewees or read with understanding literary sources. If such techniques are to be employed then they will largely determine the choice of country in which the study will take place. Successful interviewing and data collection from literary sources demand far more than the limited attainments inherent within suggestions for 'survival French' or 'survival German'. It is the human interaction between the pupil and the foreigner which is the most significant purpose of any study visit and this applies whatever the particular emphasis of any study visit, whether the focus is upon economic, social, political or cultural phenomena. To travel to a foreign country and not meet some of the people of that country is to miss the essence of a foreign *educational* visit.

In the Classroom

It is commonplace to draw a distinction between expository teaching modes, or didactic teaching, in which the teacher determines what pupils must know and how they will go about acquiring knowledge, and enquiry-based modes in which the pupils are guided by the teacher but the modes of enquiry are determined largely by the pupils. In a single lesson a teacher may employ both modes at different times and it is doubtful if teachers can be easily divided into types categorized by these modes.

Didactic modes are referred to, often pejoratively, as 'chalk and talk' or 'traditional'. They fit into the classical ideology referred to in Chapter 1. Some would view them as subject-centred or teacher-centred, but obviously a teacher who uses them would argue that they are child-centred since they are most appropriate, in his professional judgement, for the pupils in their particular situation. The distinction between pupil-centred and teacher-centred teaching is not a particularly helpful one.

When teaching didactically a teacher may utilize a variety of teaching aids including television broadcasts, radio broadcasts, 16mm films, transparencies and filmstrips. These aids may be used to supplement the class textbook. It is the textbook which has prompted much criticism of didactic methods. While textbooks are soon out-dated and often circumscribe a pupil's learning they are popular among teachers and pupils. Teachers have a love-hate relationship with textbooks—they demand them as loudly as they criticize them. Indeed some teachers have suggested that European Studies courses would be far more widespread if good textbooks were available at reasonable prices. The response of publishers to the need of teachers for suitable textbooks can be gauged by reference to the *European Studies Teachers Handbook* and its supplements (Freeman 1970).

It would be wrong to suggest that didactic methods are ineffective as techniques for transmitting information. The effectiveness is difficult to measure in general terms since each teacher who employs them will have established his own aims and objectives. For many teachers inadequate resources and inappropriate classroom accommodation ensure that didactic methods must be employed even though the teacher's personal disposition is towards more open teaching modes.

The term 'reflective' is employed to define the teaching which is different in most respects from the didactic. Massialas and Cox (1966) have summarized the reflective process: 'in short, the distinguishing character of the reflective process lies mainly in the effective combination of democratic climate, hypothesis-focused enquiry, and the functional use of facts in support of hypotheses'.

An example of a European Studies course founded in a democratic climate and underpinned by enquiry methods is the sixth-form course described by Eileen Daffern (1972). The course, bearing the title 'European Integration', was followed by grammar school sixth formers as part of a minority time general studies programme. A summary of the teaching methods employed is given in Fig. 4.

The essence of the course is the completion by the pupils of work-sheets prepared by the teacher. To answer the questions on the worksheets the pupils needed to consult publications and visual materials most of which were purchased or prepared specifically for the course. Daffern acknowledged the support she received in accumulating appropriate resources from outside agencies, in particular the Schools Information Unit of the Centre for Contemporary European Studies at the University of Sussex which was situated conveniently near her school. The growth of teachers' centres and the expansion of resource centres in secondary schools permit similar teaching ventures to be developed in other schools (Schools Council 1972b, Beswick 1975).

Daffern suggests that the following skills are necessary for the teacher engaged in a course such as hers: (a) skill as a provider of source materials; (b) skill as an observer and unobtrusive guide; (c) skill as a catalyst ('a leader of group discussion, not a strong leader with preconceived ideas but rather a "non-directive" leader, skilled in analysis and synthesis in a discussion group, able to draw on everyone's ideas, encouraging the shy, tactfully curbing the over-talkative, able to keep a main direction of thought, to open up new ones at the right moment and to bring together all ideas finally into some form of conclusion.')

The course was divided into five parts or units and each of these was studied through the use of a number of carefully prepared worksheets containing questions and problems directly related to the resource materials on the one hand and pupils' expressed interests on the other.

Daffern's course exemplifies and amplifies theoretical statements which have sought to define reflective methods of teaching. Massialas

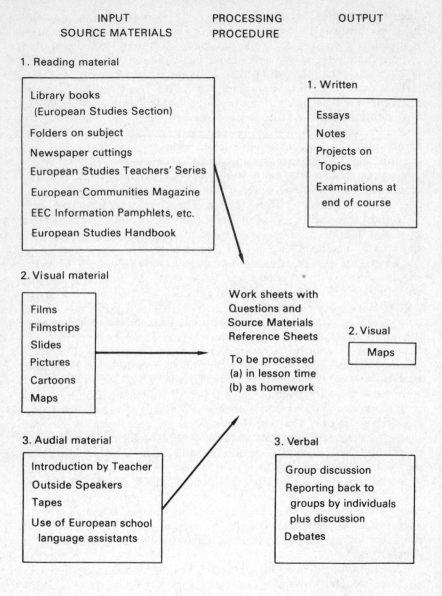

Fig. 4. Diagram used by Daffern to summarize the teaching methods employed in her 'European Integration' Course

and Cox (1966) proposed the sequence: orientation, hypothesis, exploration, evidence and generalization. Crabtree (1967) identified the following sequence:

1 Raising inquiry and achieving focus;
2 Hypothesizing relationships;
3 Verifying a pattern of association;
4 Formulating a 'knowledge-claim';
5 Revising and verifying a generalization.

The impact of theories such as these can be seen clearly in a more recent British publication (DES 1972) where the contrast between traditional and reflective modes has been summarized in two diagrams which have been designed particularly for geography teachers in secondary schools. (See Fig. 5.)

It is significant that Daffern's pupils worked mainly as individuals completing worksheets or writing projects. In similar circumstances some teachers would have favoured group methods. Confusion has arisen in the minds of some teachers over the question 'is the grouping

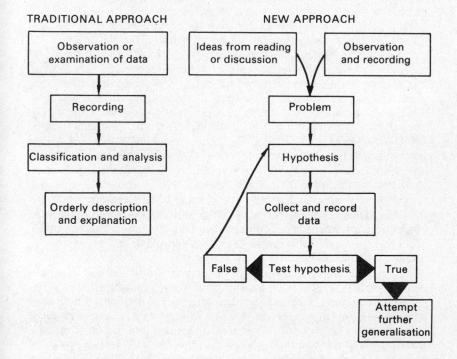

Fig. 5

of pupils in a classroom designed principally as a social control measure or is it a means of achieving better intellectual performances from all the members of a class?' These two aims frequently overlap.

Children may be grouped according to various criteria including sex, alphabetical order, defined abilities and behavioural characteristics. The sizes of groups also vary. Frequently groups are allocated topics to study and no attempt is made to distinguish between easy and more difficult topics which are then allocated to groups which may be arranged by ability. Resource materials are provided for the groups and the end-product of the group activity is often a display of charts, maps and written accounts.

A much-quoted example of this kind of group work is the study of transport, which conveniently divides into air, road, rail, inland waterways and sea transport. These aspects can be studied in the context of a single country or on a regional or continental base. Similar approaches can be used for the study of tourism, farming, or urban life in capital cities. These may be studied by taking the topic and selecting five or six countries for study and then allocating each country to a particular group for intensive investigation.

The success of teaching children in groups is determined by numerous factors including the interest generated by the topics to be studied, the appropriateness of classroom furniture for group work methods, the availability of suitable reference materials, and the skill of the teacher in defining worthwhile tasks and providing help and guidance for individuals or groups experiencing difficulties. For teachers faced with mixed ability classes the grouping of children may appear an attractive solution to a difficult teaching problem (Davies 1974, Kelly 1974 and 1975). The most disturbing feature of group teaching for the sensitive teacher is that it highlights individual difficulties which may be hidden in class teaching. While the teacher should know about the difficulties, having discovered them he may not be able to solve them. Children with learning difficulties often become the group artists, tracing maps and diagrams, shading and colouring, but never approaching the problems besetting the more able members of the groups. These children require considerable help, the help of the 'unobtrusive guide' referred to by Daffern.

Group teaching is unlikely to be employed throughout a whole course. At its best it provides an opportunity for pupils to practise skills which have already been acquired by more formal methods. These may include interpreting foreign maps, photographs, and statistical information; constructing statistical diagrams; reading and under-standing documents and newspaper cuttings; abstracting extracts from novels and plays and relating them to situations in real life. These and other skills can be brought together in the classroom to solve problems.

They must be carefully taught to ensure that pupils are adept in their use.

Simulations and educational games are increasingly popular activities in some school subjects and seem to have considerable potential for European Studies courses.

In a simulation exercise pupils are encouraged to take on clearly defined roles which they perform as if in real life. Successful simulation is achieved when pupils understand their roles and the situation which confronts them. Clarke (1973) has defined the advantages and limitations of a simulation. The advantages are

1 it is highly motivating;
2 it allows both bright and less bright pupils to participate;
3 it gives practice in decision making;
4 it is not teacher dominated;
5 it encourages creativity and independent thinking.

The limitations are

1 it may be time-consuming;
2 some simulations turn into entertainment;
3 some pupils confuse the simulation with reality.

While role-playing and simulation may be conceived of as an ad hoc activity emerging spontaneously from the subject matter of a particular lesson, a simulation which involves the interaction of pupils playing various roles requires careful preparation. In a simulation the pupils are asked to step into someone else's shoes, indeed the pupil is really being asked to think his way into the mind of someone and this adoption of a role demands that the pupil should understand thoroughly the lifestyle of the person he is playing. The situations too must be understood to the extent that the simulation can proceed without constant interruption by the teacher. Interruptions to explain details of role or situation or correct what would appear to be errors in interpretation are likely to ruin the flow of the simulation. In addition to preparing the pupils thoroughly for the simulation, and defining the roles and the situation the teacher must pay particular attention to the allocation of roles to individual pupils. The danger of the most articulate, persuasive pupil dominating a simulation and perhaps making more of a role than the situation demands is a serious one. Simulations are a means to an end and the end is a step forward by the pupils in their understanding of a particular human situation. Pupils may through a simulation learn more about each other than about the situation being simulated and while this may have merit in some classrooms it is something which a teacher must allow for when allocating roles.

Educational games can be seen as a development of simulations. They have become an acceptable method of teaching in geography, history and economics in secondary schools and they have a valuable contribution to make to the effective teaching of European Studies. Designing educational games requires considerable skill on the part of the teacher though he may receive much helpful advice and examples of tested games from authors such as Tansey (1971), Walford (1969), Dalton et al. (1972) and Elliott et al. (1975). In essence an educational game presents pupils with a competitive situation in which the winners are those who apply knowledge and skills most successfully. Needless to say the knowledge and the skills must first be acquired by the participants and the game may be considered as a sophisticated testing device which ensures that the pupils can use their learned knowledge and skills in a carefully structured and controlled situation.

Educational games focus on situations which are rooted in the real world but have been simplified in order to highlight particular problems which can be resolved by individuals or groups of pupils generally working in a classroom. The problems must be capable of solution by the pupils and it is the teacher's task to ensure that in selecting or designing a game it is appropriate to the level of attainment of the class. Advocates of educational games see them as a means of motivating young people to study and see them as informal and pleasurable activities which yield a variety of products some of which are derived from the pupils' grasp of models and concepts and others from aspects of social control and class morale. Because European Studies courses are frequently justified on the ground that they promote social awareness and lead to a greater understanding of Europeans and the problems they are facing games based on these in which the pupils play the role of people from other countries seem to present one of the most profitable directions for advance in teaching methods.

CHAPTER SIX

Approaches and Resources

European Studies syllabuses are usually presented as a list of major themes which are then subdivided into smaller topics. It is customary to assume that a syllabus is not a teaching scheme and that it should not determine the sequence in which themes should be studied. In planning a course a teacher must decide the sequence of themes, perhaps in consultation with his pupils, and he would need to structure the work of a single term, a year or two years so that related themes were taught close to each other and that more difficult themes may come later in the course rather than earlier. An attempt to structure the teaching of a two-year course for secondary school pupils aged 14-16 years is given in this outline.

COURSE OUTLINE FOR A TWO-YEAR EUROPEAN STUDIES COURSE FOR SCHOOL LEAVERS

YEAR ONE

Winter Term

Week

1 *INTRODUCTION*
   Physical Features of the
   Continent: location of nations,
   selected capitals

2 *POPULATION*
   Continental Distribution

3 Changes in Population: death
   rates and birth rates, age
   pyramids

4 Emigration and Immigration

5 Effects of War

6 ⎱ Regional Centres of Population
7 ⎰ Population Centres—case studies
8 ⎱ of selected cities: Brussels,
9 ⎰ Berlin, Moscow, Stockholm and
   Venice

Winter Term, contd.

Week

10 *RICH AND POOR REGIONS*
    Continental Distribution

11 ⎱ Case Studies of Declining
12 ⎰ Regions: Italian Mezzogiorno,
    Brittany, Wallonia

13 ⎱ Case Studies of Growth Regions:
14 ⎰ Randstad Holland, Central
    Sweden, Northern Italy

Spring Term

Week

1 *EUROPEAN INDUSTRIES*
   Coal Mining

2 Iron and Steel

3 Engineering and the Aircraft
   Industry

Spring Term, contd.

Week

4 Car Industry
5 Chemical Industry
6 *ENERGY*
   Natural Gas
7 North Sea Oil
8 Thermal Energy Production
9 Hydro-Electric Power Production
10 Alternative Sources of Energy
11 The Energy Crisis
12 *INDUSTRIAL ORGANIZATION*
   Small-scale Private Industry
13 Nationalized Industries
14 Multi-National Companies

Summer Term

Week

1 *AGRICULTURE*
   Agricultural Distribution
2 Climate, Soils and Agriculture
3 Case Studies of Farming:
   Subsistence
4 Commercial Grain Farming
5 Viticulture
6 Horticulture
7 Co-operative Farming
8 Collective Farming
9 Transhumance and Nomadic Herding
10 Rural Settlements

YEAR TWO

Winter Term

Week

1 *ENVIRONMENTAL PROBLEMS*
   River and Sea Pollution
2 Forestry *v.* Agriculture
3 Recreation and Leisure
4 *TOURISM*
   Case Studies of Coastal Areas
5 Case Studies of Lake Areas
6 Case Studies of Mountain Areas
7 *TRANSPORT*
   Road and Rail
8 Canals and Coastal Shipping
9 Ports and Airports
10 *POLITICAL LIFE*
   Nations and Frontiers
11 The Iron Curtain
12 Political Institutions: forms of government
13 Political Ideas: Democracy
14 Totalitarianism

Spring Term

Week

1 Postwar Crises: Berlin, Hungary, Czechoslovakia
2 Cyprus, Portugal, Northern Ireland

Spring Term, contd.

Week

3 *INTERNATIONAL ORGANIZATIONS*
   Council of Europe
4 NATO and the Warsaw Pact
5 The EEC: Origins
6 The EEC: Structure
7 The EEC: Policies
8 International Trade
9 Changes in the Pattern of Trade
10 The Problem of Inflation
11 Standards of Living
12 Costs of Living
13 *SOCIAL LIFE IN EUROPE*
   Education
14 Problems of Old Age

Summer Term

Week

1 Role of Women
2 Crime
3 Legal Systems
4 Trade Unions and Business Organizations
5 *REVISION AND EXAMINATIONS*

In the following pages nine themes which are included commonly in syllabuses and course outlines have been selected and for each theme a conceptual structure has been designed to serve as a guide for the selection of topics to incorporate into a course. By specifying ten key questions for each theme it is hoped that guidance will be given as to the *highest* level of understanding which pupils and teachers should seek to attain through the study of the theme.

Although the provision of teaching materials, especially textbooks and broadcast materials, is steadily improving it must be acknowledged that in most instances teachers are devising their own teaching materials and they are heavily dependent on books written at levels well beyond that of the pupils who are generally taught European Studies. Preparing guides to teaching resources for European Studies is not an easy task. Undoubtedly, the most useful guidance for teachers has been supplied by the Centre for Contemporary European Studies at the University of Sussex in the *Handbook for European Studies* and its supplements together with the reviews which are published in the Centre's periodical, *Teaching about Europe*. It is partly in response to the resources problem that groups of teachers have been meeting in local teachers' centres to share ideas and devise teaching materials and, as a result of these self-help activities, some schools have been able to obtain a variety of customer-designed curriculum materials.

It is always difficult to prepare lists of materials for other teachers to use for the obvious reason that books rapidly become outdated and also because people's judgement of books will differ. It is with these provisos to the fore that the lists in this chapter have been prepared.

Population

European Studies are predominantly social studies. This is reflected in the emphasis given by teachers in their courses to the conditions and problems of people within Europe. The study of population, therefore, has considerable importance within a European Studies course. Commonly, European Studies syllabuses contain references to such themes or topics as immigrants, rural depopulation, urbanization, the European family and the place of women in society. By preparing a conceptual diagram, such as the network in Fig. 6 it is possible to illustrate how some of these themes overlap and connect under the general heading 'Population'. Clearly population is far more complicated, interesting and dynamic than a simple map identification exercise in which pupils look at a map of a particular country and then locate its capital city, before finding out the country's total population.

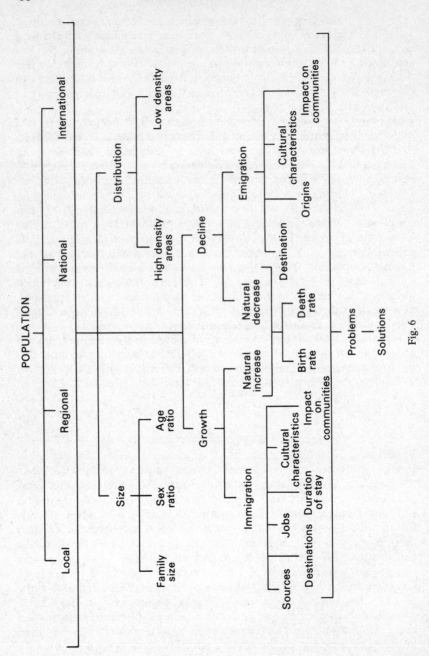

Fig. 6

References

Böhning, R., *Migration of Workers in the United Kingdom and the European Community*, Oxford University Press for the Institute of Race Relations
Castles, S. and Kosack, G., *Immigrant Workers and Class Structures in Western Europe*, Oxford University Press
Clarke, J. I., *Population Geography*, Pergamon
Classen, L. H. and Dreux, P., *Migration Policy in Europe: A Comparative Study*, Heath
Deakin, N. (ed.), *Immigrants in Europe*, Fabian Society
Kosinski, L. A., *The Population of Europe*, Longman
Kosinski, L. A. and Prothero, R. M., *People on the Move: Studies on Internal Migration*, Methuen
Zelinsky, W., *Prologue to Population Geography*, Prentice-Hall

Key Questions

1   Where are the regions of highest population density in Europe? Do these regions overlap national frontiers? How are they related to the distribution of natural resources, food supplies and communications?

2   Which European countries or groups of countries have growing populations and which have declining populations and what are the reasons for these trends?

3   What are the economic, political and social implications of differences in the age ratios and sex ratios between countries? How can countries change these ratios if such changes were considered desirable?

4   What are the links between a nation's total population and its international political influence?

5   Which nations suffered the most serious losses of population during the second world war? How have these losses been compensated for in the post-war period?

6   What problems are encountered in calculating the national sizes of population? Why are accurate census figures important?

7   What measures can national governments introduce to alter the population figures within their national frontiers? To what extent are national frontiers population control devices?

8   Should freedom of movement be an international human right?

9   Which European countries have the largest number of immigrants? From which countries and continents have they travelled? Who are they and how long do they usually stay? Where do they live? What particular social problems do they experience and how are these being solved?

10   From which European countries are large numbers of people emigrating? What are the effects on the communities left behind? What are the reactions of the countries which are losing population through emigration? Who are the emigrants in terms of age, sex, education and social group?

Cities and Urbanization

In Chapter 2 urbanization is linked with industrialization as one of the proposed 'central, unavoidable themes' in the study of Europe. Basically, there are three approaches to the study of urban areas. First, the planning approach in which cities are considered as structures with distinctive forms and zones which can be classified and used as a basis for comparative studies. Urban geographers utilize this approach and they distinguish central business districts, urban cores and suburban zones. They have also elaborated theories of urban form. Second, the broadly social approach in which the emphasis is upon the social problems generated by urban growth: the problems of the homeless, the aged, ethnic and cultural minorities, communications, traffic and crime. Third, the historical approach in which the focus is upon the evolution of selected European cities. This traces the growth and decline of cities in particular historical areas and links cities with the cultural conditions prevailing in the regions and nations in which the cities are located. The choice of cities for study will be largely determined by the approach a teacher decides to adopt. A case can be made for the study of every city in Europe. Figure 7 is intended to provide some guidance as to the criteria which may be used in the selection of examples.

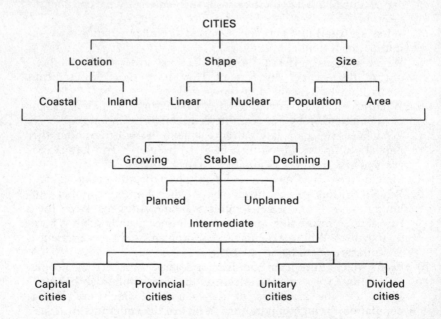

References

Benkinsale, P. and Houston, J. M. (eds.), *Urbanization and its Problems*, Blackwell
Berry, B., *The Human Consequences of Urbanization*, Macmillan
Burke, G. L., *Greenheart Metropolis*, Macmillan
Dickinson, R., *The West European City*, Routledge & Kegan Paul
Fuerst, J. S., *Public Housing in Europe and America*, Croom Helm
Geddes, P., *Cities in Evolution*, Benn
Hall, P., *The World Cities*, World University Press
Hall, P., *Urban and Regional Planning*, Penguin
Holliday, J., *Cities and City Regions in Europe*, Lanchester Polytechnic
Le Corbusier, *The Radiant City*, Faber
Merlin, P., *New Towns*, Methuen
Robson, W. A. and Regan, D. E., *The Great Cities of the World*, Allen & Unwin

Key Questions

1 What were the distinctive characteristics of selected European cities before the industrial revolution? Where were cities concentrated in Europe before 1800?

2 How do capital cities differ from provincial cities in selected European countries?

3 What influence have the planners Howard, Geddes, Soria y Mata and Le Corbusier had upon the design of European cities?

4 How widespread are new towns in Europe? How far have they contributed to the solution of urban problems in Sweden, France, the Netherlands and Russia?

5 What measures have been taken by governments to control the expansion of cities? How far is the French centralization problem, summarized in the expression 'le désert français', a European problem?

6 Why should life in capital cities be considered atypical of the way of life in the nations in which they are situated?

7 Which aspects of cities should be conserved when massive urban redevelopment takes place?

8 Why is it claimed that urban motorways and the construction of tower blocks in large cities create more problems than they solve?

9 Why are Berlin, Brussels and Belfast described as 'divided cities'? How can the divisions be healed?

10 Is the increasing concentration of the population of Europe into a number of cities inevitable?

Problem Regions

Whatever criteria we employ to distinguish between rich and poor regions in Europe it is possible to define groups of nations which are relatively rich and others which are relatively poor, and within any one nation we can discern regions which are poor and regions which are rich. The European Community defined three types of problem region—frontier regions, regions with declining industries, and regions experiencing rural depopulation. This classification, though based on the EEC as it was up to 1972 can be extended to the whole of Europe. In deciding how to teach about problem regions a teacher has a number of choices in the main aspects to emphasize. He may begin with case studies of families selected from contrasting or comparable regions or he may start with extracts from recent newspaper articles describing policies under discussion or being introduced by governments or international organizations to solve certain regional problems. There are several popular regions including the Mezzogiorno, the Ruhr, northern Scandinavia and Brittany. Significantly these are all from the non-Communist states of Europe. A possible structure for defining problem regions for study is shown in Fig. 8.

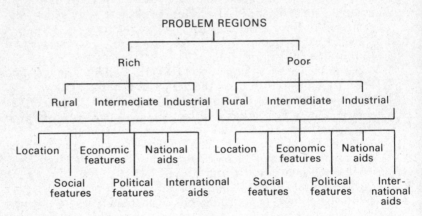

Fig. 8

References

Hamilton, F. E. I., *Yugoslavia: Patterns of Economic Activity*, Bell
Hansen, N. M., *French Regional Planning*, Edinburgh University Press
Knowles, R. and Stowe, P. W. E., *Europe in Maps, Books 1 and 2*, Longman
Lind, H. and Flockton, C., *Regional Planning in Britain and the Six*, PEP
PEP, *Economic Planning and Policies in Britain, France and Germany*
Scargill, D. I. (ed.), *Problem Regions of Europe*, Oxford University Press. The following titles have been published to date.
    Burtenshaw, D., *Saar-Lorraine*
    Clout, H. D., *The Massif Central*
    Hamilton, F. E. I., *Poland's Western and Northern Territories*
    Hamilton, F. E. I., *The Moscow City Region*
    Hellen, J. A., *North Rhine-Westphalia*
    Lawrence, G. R. P., *Randstad Holland*
    Lichtenberger, E., *The Eastern Alps*
    Mead, W. R., *The Scandinavian Northlands*

Mountjoy, A. B., *The Mezzogiorno*
Naylon, J., *Andalusia*
Smith, J. L., *Western Peninsulas of Europe*
Thompson, I. B., *The Lower Rhone and Marseille*
Thompson, I. B., *The Paris Basin*

Key Questions

1 To what extent are regional problems within any one European country international problems?
2 What criteria can be employed to distinguish rich and poor regions? Must a rich region contain a wealth of natural resources?
3 Is there a correlation between accessible energy resources and rich regions?
4 What different solutions must be applied to the problems of poor agricultural regions and poor industrial regions? What success have European nations attained in solving the problems of both kinds of region?
5 Is there a good argument for allowing poor agricultural regions to continue to decline so permitting a greater availability of land for recreational use?
6 Why are enormous efforts being made to reclaim land in some countries which have declining rural regions?
7 What is the role of multinational companies in the revitalization of declining industrial regions? How do national governments seek to attract these companies?
8 What are the differences between eastern and western European countries in the measures introduced to solve regional problems?
9 What does the term 'industrial inertia' mean? How far does this account for the decline of industrial regions?
10 What are the links between rural depopulation, emigration, immigration and the emergence of problem regions?

Rural Life

The significance of agriculture varies from country to country within Europe, but even in those countries which have experienced massive urbanization rural life and traditions are still important in defining the way of life and the cultural traditions of the population as a whole. The interpenetration of the rural and urban communities is a theme worth exploring in itself. Under the heading of rural life three broad themes have been identified and illustrated in Fig. 9. Without a clear understanding of the organization of individual farms it is unlikely that farming systems can be understood and the study of farming systems provides the key to the understanding of farming communities. These three components must be considered in the context of the physical and human environments in which they are located. A problem emerges in selecting what might be considered as typical farms and associated farming systems and communities. Thus, if French rural life is to be studied, is a vineyard in the Loire Valley a better starting point than a grain farm in the Paris Basin or a subsistence farm in Brittany? It can be argued that without an awareness of the differences inherent in these three examples a child is unlikely to understand the characteristics of the French peasantry. An understanding of rural life in Europe is interesting and important for its own sake but it also has the value of providing insight into the literature, art and music as well as the economic and political lives of European states.

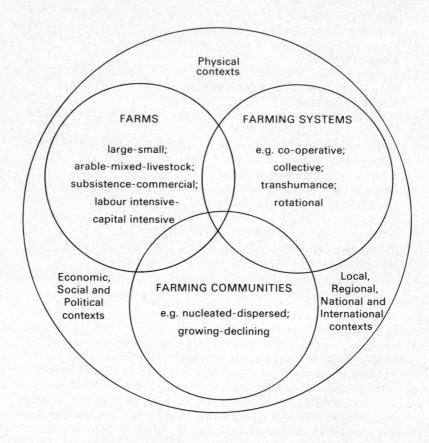

Fig. 9

References

Chisholm, M., *Rural Settlement and Land Use*, Hutchinson
Clout, H. D., *Agriculture*, Macmillan
Clout, H. D., *Rural Geography: An Introductory Survey*, Pergamon
Franklin, S. H., *Rural Societies*, Macmillan
Franklin, S. H., *The European Peasantry*, Methuen
King, R., *Land Reform: The Italian Experience*, Butterworth
Marsh, J. and Ritson, C., *Agricultural Policy and the Common Market*, PEP
Mayhew, A., *Rural Settlement and Farming in Germany*, Batsford
Morin, E., *Plodémet*, Allen Lane, the Penguin Press
Simmons, I. G., *Rural Recreation in the Industrial World*, Edward Arnold
Symons, L. J., *Russian Agriculture: A Geographic Survey*, Bell
Trow-Smith, R., *Life from the Land: the Growth of Farming in Western Europe*, Longman

Key Questions

1   Are physical factors—relief, climate, soils—more important in determining farming patterns in Europe than human and political factors?
2   What significant differences are there between systems of land ownership among nations in northern, eastern, western and southern Europe?
3   What are the main differences between co-operative and collective farming?
4   How are rural villages changing in character? Are any of the major recent changes improvements on the character of villages?
5   How important are festivals and holidays in the lives of villagers?
6   Does tourism threaten or support the lives of rural communities?
7   To be profitable must European farms be large farms?
8   Why is it more difficult to introduce international agricultural policies than it is to introduce industrial policies?
9   How do patterns of rural settlement differ from country to country within regions of Europe?
10 What techniques are employed to portray rural land use accurately on maps in various countries? What are the difficulties commonly found in collecting the data for these maps and in interpreting them?

Transport and Communications
The interest of modern language teachers in preparing their pupils for cross-Channel journeys has ensured that a strong emphasis has been given to transport in European Studies courses. While the details of passenger journeys, including passports, the careful reading of timetables and the relative speeds of hovercraft, cross-Channel car ferries and charter aircraft, may be of interest to the potential holidaymaker, other aspects of transport and communications are also

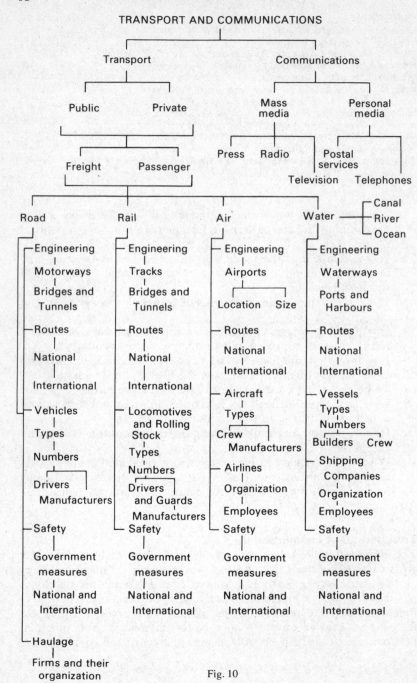

Fig. 10

worthy of consideration. The diagram (Fig. 10) indicates the possible content of each of the major forms of transport, and suggests the possible inter-relationships between the various items which appear under the major headings. Since transport and communications provide the means whereby people and ideas move from country to country they are of importance in any European Studies course. It is in the streets, airports and docks of Britain and in the television programmes and sporting exchanges that many pupils are likely to notice the obvious links between Britain and her neighbours on mainland Europe. Proximity, accessibility and interdependence are three of the major concepts which are likely to emerge from the study of transport and communications in European Studies.

References
Despicht, N., *Policies for Transport in the Common Market*, Lombard Press
Despicht, N., *The Transport Policy of the European Communities*, PEP
Symons, L. and White, C., *Russian Transport*, Bell
PEP, *Regional Management of the Rhine*, Papers of a Chatham House Study Group

Key Questions
1 What are the disadvantages associated with the improvement in forms of transport?
2 Why are inland waterways more important in the internal transport facilities of some countries than others?
3 What transport problems have been created by the establishment of the Iron Curtain? What difficulties are encountered by travellers who wish to cross this frontier?
4 What safety measures should be applied to all private cars in Europe? How could such measures be introduced and enforced? Which nations have the most detailed safety codes?
5 Why are transport industries often nationalized by governments in Europe? What are the difficulties involved in private enterprise transport?
6 What are the difficulties faced in the provision of international television programmes? Is there a case for having an EEC television and radio service?
7 Do all transport improvements produce environmental problems?
8 What are the factors which hinder the development of a European motorways network?
9 Why do the Scandinavian countries have a single international airline? What are the advantages and disadvantages of such international co-operation?
10 Should the various forms of transport compete with each other for business?

Education

In applying the generally accepted principle of moving from the known to the unknown teachers and pupils are likely to find the study of European educational institutions particularly interesting. There is a fascination in learning the length of the school terms and days, the subjects studied, the types of punishment in use, the range of extra-curricular activities, even the types of school meals in various countries. Since most language teachers are likely to have spent a period of time in either a French or German school as part of their degree or certificate studies they are likely to be well-informed about the organization of a particular school. The teacher's task is to extend this experience into other countries and other institutions to provide a comparative study to enable the pupil to place his British experience and knowledge into a broader setting. There is a danger that in the study of institutions arid

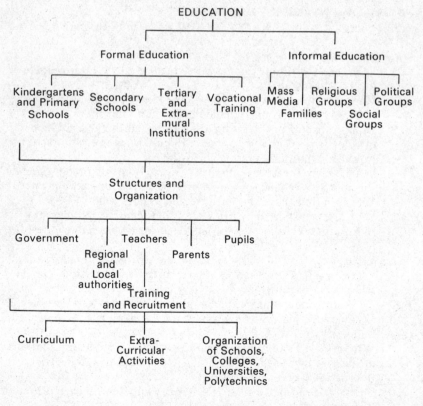

Fig. 11

and uninteresting organizational details will be stressed. Case studies derived either from school-to-school exchanges or pupil-to-pupil pen-pal arrangements can be effectively used to breathe life into such studies.

References

Council for Cultural Co-operation of the Council of Europe, *School Systems: a Study Guide*, Council of Europe

Friedmann, F. G., *Youth and Society*, Macmillan

Jansen, S., *Possible Futures of European Education* (Plan Europe 2000), Martin Nijhoff

King, E., Moor, C. and Mundy, J., *Post-compulsory Education: A New Analysis in Western Europe*, Sage

OECD, *Reviews of National Policies for Education*

Poignant, R., *Education in the Industrialised Countries* (Plan Europe 2000), Martin Nijhoff

School of Barbiana, *Letter to a Teacher*, Penguin

Tomiak, J. J., *Education in the Soviet Union*, David & Charles

Vaizey, J., *Education*, Macmillan

Key Questions

1 Why is so much emphasis placed on the concept of life-long education ('éducation permanente')?

2 Account for the link between religious bodies and schools in selected western European countries.

3 Why do some European countries place greater emphasis on vocational secondary education than others? Are there differences between countries in the provision of vocational education for girls?

4 Why have international and European schools been established? What are their distinctive features?

5 Account for the differences in the language policies of selected European countries. How do the language policies in Eastern Europe differ from those in the West?

6 What special provisions have been made to assist immigrants educationally in Europe? How successful have these measures been?

7 How widespread is comprehensive secondary education in Europe? What differences are there in the lengths of compulsory schooling between countries?

8 What influences have the Council of Europe and the EEC had upon the educational systems and educational practice in their member states?

9 Is there such a thing as a 'European youth culture'? If so, what are its distinctive characteristics and how can these be explained?

10 Why do educational systems differ so much between neighbouring countries?

Nations and Nationalism

In selecting topics for study in a European Studies course a decision has to be taken as to the geographical area on which to base the topic. It is possible to base a whole course on a series of case studies selected from various parts of Europe. It is also possible to deal with topics on a continental basis. Most commonly, certain basic physical features—notably relief and climate—are taught on a continental basis and human phenomena, especially studies of ways of life, are considered on a national basis. There is obviously a danger in over-emphasizing the nation-state in that too much attention may be given to national differences by searching for national oddities and idiosyncrasies and insufficient attention paid to the more generalized European themes. When European Studies is referred to as a comparative study the comparisons and contrasts are usually drawn between nations. Advocates of French Studies and German Studies argue that it is better to know a single nation (or language community?) well rather than to know a group of nations or a whole continent in broad terms. From Fig. 12 it is possible to detect the complications inherent in the selection of features which give some understanding of another nation. It could well be argued that the level of success of a teacher in dealing with the study of nations and nationalism determines the success or failure of a European Studies course.

References

The 'How They Live and Work' series published by David and Charles, e.g. Irwin, J. L., *The Finns and Lapps;* Spencer, A., *The Norwegians*
Knapp, W., *Unity and Nationalism in Europe since 1945*, Pergamon
Wallace, H., *National Governments and the European Communities*, PEP
A Survey of Europe Today, Reader's Digest Association

Key Questions

1 What are the distinctive characteristics of a nation? What are the differences between a nation-state, a nation, a tribe and a community?
2 Which European nations are found in more than one country?
3 Are separatist groups in Europe groups of nationalists?
4 What are the differences between patriots and nationalists?
5 Many nations in Europe achieved political independence in relatively recent times. How were nation-states created? In what circumstances have nation-states been divided or joined together?
6 What are the constructive, positive aspects of nationalism?
7 Is it possible for some nation-states to be more nationalistic than others?
8 To understand what life is like in a foreign country is it really necessary to understand the language of the country?

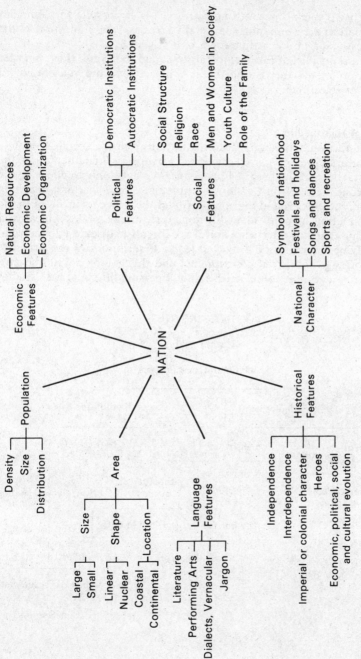

Fig. 12

9   What is meant by a 'strong country'? Is it possible for countries small in area to be internationally strong? How important is the possession of a coastline for a nation-state?

10 Draw up a list of European countries and then rank them in order of preference for visiting them. What criteria did you employ in your selection?

Political Institutions

The interaction between political institutions and the social, economic and cultural lives of the countries of Europe is fundamental to the understanding of the lives of Europeans. We have only to consider the significance of the Iron Curtain to appreciate this. The main teaching problem revolves around the complexity of the concepts involved in the understanding of political institutions. Historical, philosophical and economic elements intertwine and it is difficult to disentangle them. In simplifying the issues we are often led to descriptions of the structure and workings of selected governments and this can be a dull and arid exercise. Biographies of selected political personalities and case studies

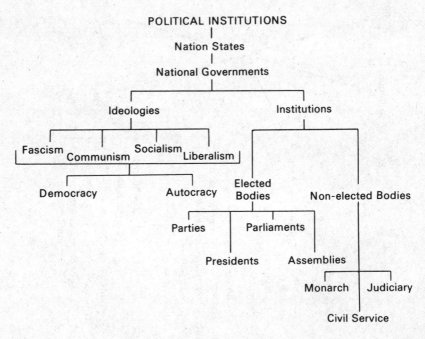

Fig. 13

of problems which were resolved by political action allow the human elements to dominate the structural elements. Undoubtedly, without an understanding of the political institutions in particular countries the pupils will have a very limited appreciation of the issues involved in the discussion of city life, farming, pollution, regional problems and the formation of international institutions. Any comparison of life in eastern Europe with life in Scandinavia or western Europe is likely to be seriously impaired without an understanding of the relevant institutions.

References

Avril, P., *Politics in France*, Penguin
Calvocoressi, P., *World Politics Since 1945*, Longman
Cook, C. and Paxton, J., *European Political Facts 1918-1973*, Macmillan
Gregory, D., *Mussolini and the Fascist Era*, Edward Arnold
Heater, D. B., *Political Ideas in the Modern World*, Harrap
Henig, S. and Pinder, J., *European Political Parties*, Allen & Unwin (PEP)
Holt, S., *Six European States: The Countries of the European Community and their Political Systems*, Hamish Hamilton
Ionescu, G., *The Politics of the European Communist States*, Weidenfeld & Nicolson
Ionescu, G., *The New Politics of European Integration*, Macmillan
Kedward, H. R., *Fascism*, Blackie
Lakeman, E., *Nine Democracies, Electoral Systems of the Countries of the EEC*, Electoral Reform Society
Ray, J., *Hitler and Mussolini*, Heinemann Educational Books
Savage, K., *Marxism and Communism*, Bodley Head
Smith, D., *Left and Right in Twentieth Century Europe*, Longman

Key Questions

1 What do the political terms 'left', 'right' and 'centre' mean? How do the definitions vary between eastern and western Europe, and between individual countries in western Europe?

2 Why is the referendum used more frequently in some countries than others?

3 What significant differences are there in the electoral systems employed within countries forming the EEC and between eastern and western European countries? How important is voting in the political lives of selected European countries? Are all Europeans eligible to vote in national elections at the age of eighteen?

4 Is it possible to compare the roles of monarchs and presidents in western European countries?

5 What is meant by the term 'political stability'? What do post-war crises in such countries as Greece, Hungary, Cyprus, Czechoslovakia, France, Northern Ireland and Spain teach us about political stability?

6 How important is ideology in the understanding of the political organization of selected European countries?

7 'Guilty until you are proved innocent' and 'Innocent until you are proved guilty'. Which of these two basic principles is most frequently used in European legal systems?
8 What are the significant differences between the post-1945 political histories of the Scandinavian and the Mediterranean states?
9 What is the connection between a nation's political system and a nation's economic system? What is the political role of the military in selected European countries?
10 Is the strengthening of local and regional government a common trend in Europe? Why is strong, centralized government so frequently criticized?

International Institutions

Britain's entry into the EEC has been one of the major generating forces behind the emergence of European Studies courses in schools. Not surprisingly, therefore, most syllabuses include some reference to the movement towards political unification in post-1945 Europe. For this movement to be properly understood attention must be given to other international institutions which have had powerful influences on European life. The institutions referred to in Fig. 14 have a political flavour and it would be wrong to suggest that these are the only important international institutions active in contemporary Europe.

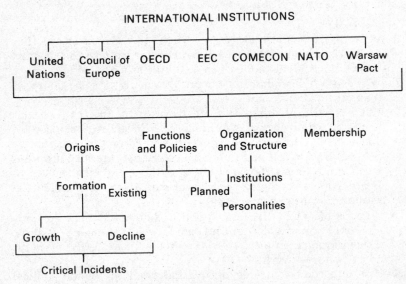

Fig. 14

Such diverse organizations as the Red Cross, the International Broadcasting Union and the Olympic Committee could also have been included. The study of international institutions enables the pupil to place regional and national topics or themes in an international setting. One of the dangers is that International Institutions, like political institutions, will be treated as a distinct topic to be dealt with in a series of lessons whereas it could be incorporated into many other themes and it could provide the link between such themes as agriculture, industry, transport and trade. If international institutions are really significant in the daily lives of Europeans it is difficult to see how daily lives can be discussed without some reference to the influence of the institutions. As was mentioned on page 74 there is always the problem when studying institutions of emphasizing the structural aspects of institutions. Some teachers may hesitate when dealing with some of the controversial aspects of political institutions, national or international, but this problem is one which permeates every aspect of European Studies.

References

Albrecht-Carrié, R., *The Unity of Europe: an Historical Survey*, Secker & Warburg
Barraclough, G., *European Unity in Thought and Action*, Blackwell
Birley, R., *The Concept of Europe*, TEAM Handbook
Chadwick, J., *International Organizations*, Methuen
Cosgrove, C. A. and Twitchett, K. J., *The New International Actors: the UN and the EEC*, Macmillan
de la Mahotière, S., *Towards One Europe*, Penguin
Galtung, J., *The European Community: A Superpower in the Making*, Allen & Unwin
Hodges, M., (ed.), *European Integration: Selected Readings*, Penguin
Kaplan, L. S. (ed.), *NATO and the Policy of Containment*, Heath
Knorr, K., *NATO, Past—Present—Prospect*, TEAM Handbook
Mellor, R. E. H., *Eastern Europe: a Geography of the COMECON Countries*, Macmillan
Niblock, M., *The EEC: National Parliaments and Community Decision Making*, PEP
Parker, G., *The Logic of Unity*, Longman
Pryce, R., *Politics of the European Community*, Butterworth
Robertson, A. H., *European Institutions: Cooperation, Integration, Unification*, Stevens, for the Institute of World Affairs
Sampson, A., *The New Europeans*, Hodder & Stoughton

Key Questions

1   In which European countries has the United Nations been most active? Which projects have been sponsored in Europe by the United Nations? How successful have these projects been?

2   Some nations such as Sweden and Switzerland have not become members of some international institutions. Why is this, and what have they gained or lost by their non-participation?

3   How 'European' are the various international institutions shown in Fig. 14? Which institutions are most active in promoting links between European and other countries?

4   What is 'détente'? Could this have been established without international institutions?

5   Why is the EEC described as an undemocratic institution? Should all international institutions be founded on direct democratic elections?

6   Which European statesmen have been most influential in promoting European unification in the twentieth century? How can their influence be assessed?

7   What does the expression 'a federal Europe' mean? Is federalism a realistic solution to Europe's political problems?

8   Has unification been more successfully achieved in eastern Europe than in western Europe? What are the political, social, economic and cultural links between eastern and western Europe?

9   Why did Britain join the EEC? For what reasons was her entry into the Communities so delayed?

10 What does a nation gain and lose by becoming a member of an international institution?

CHAPTER SEVEN

Classroom Lessons

In this chapter three lessons taken from different kinds of European Studies courses are described and discussed. The courses themselves differ since the pupils quoted are of three different kinds, 14-16 year-old pupils in a mixed-ability group, sixth formers following a CEE course, and 'new sixth formers' taking a minority time course. The lessons highlight three different styles of teaching, a didactic or instructional style, a more directly pupil-centred, resource-based style and an open-ended class simulation.

These lessons serve to bring together some of the points raised in earlier chapters with particular reference to aims and objectives, the subject matter of European Studies courses, the organization of courses in particular schools and aspects of learning and teaching.

Lesson 1   European Ways of Life: Slides and a Worksheet
The teacher, a modern languages specialist, described this class as 'mixed ability with a bias towards the lower levels of the ability scale'. The pupils are in the first term of a two-year CSE Mode 3 European Studies course. At the end of the previous year, the pupils' third in the school, they had been required to choose a number of subjects drawn from three lists and virtually all of these pupils had decided against following courses in modern languages. Pupils who chose the European Studies option were unable to study modern languages, history and geography. The European Studies course was allocated six lessons each week divided into three double lessons. The lesson described here is a double lesson in the middle of a topic entitled 'European Ways of Life'.

As soon as the thirty pupils have settled down in the untidy rows of desks the teacher informs them that he will be showing them six slides, five of which he took on a recent school visit to France. He explains that he wants the pupils to pay close attention to what he says about the slides since later in the lesson he will distribute a worksheet for them to finish and the questions on this worksheet will be directly related to the slides. The pupils are told to clear their desks of books and papers and, when reasonable order has been established, the teacher switches on the 35mm slide projector and asks a pupil to switch off the lights.

The first slide shows a family at dinner and the teacher informs the class that this is a French family at home in Paris. He draws the pupils' attention to the furniture, the cutlery, the dishes and the food. All of these features are clearly portrayed. The pupils are asked to distinguish between this 'typical French scene' and what they would consider to be the equivalent English situation.

The second slide is similar to the first one: it shows another family at dinner though this time the family is Italian. The teacher draws comparisons and contrasts between the Italian, French and English situations. The teacher summarizes the main points orally and emphasizes the constituents of the meal and how they were prepared, the distinctive national dishes of France and Italy with brief references to local variations, national festivals when special meals are eaten, and the sources of the foodstuffs, distinguishing between local and regional food supplies.

The third slide shows a Parisian street market and the focus is on a vegetable stall. The pupils are asked to identify the various vegetables and to notice the prices. The teacher moves to the blackboard and he writes a list of the vegetables and alongside some of these he records the prices as shown on the slide. Brief comments are made about French currency and the use of metric weights.

The fourth slide shows a horsemeat shop. The pupils' attention is drawn to the golden horse's head above the shop door and to the shop's name—'Boucherie Chevaline'. The teacher writes a list of six foodshops on the blackboard—grocer, greengrocer, baker, confectioner, fishmonger and butcher—and alongside them writes their French equivalents.

The inside of a modern French hypermarket is the subject of the fifth slide. The teacher explains the French tradition of small shops and then refers to a number of cities where hypermarkets have been built. He asks questions about the advantages and disadvantages for the French housewife of these establishments. He asks the pupils why hypermarkets are rare in Britain. He contrasts the third slide—the street market—with this slide of the hypermarket.

The final slide shows a pavement café. He asks the pupils to explain why these are common in France and rare in England. He draws their attention to the filter coffee. He engages briefly in role playing: he plays the parts of a customer and a waiter in a typical café scene. This is considered hilarious by some of the pupils and it concludes the slide-show. The projector is switched off, the lights are switched on, and the pupils are provided with worksheets. The teacher writes a brief summary of each of the six slides on the blackboard and the pupils are encouraged to refer to back issues of *Passport** which are piled on a desk at the front of the room. For the rest of the lesson the pupils work their way through the questions on the worksheet. The teacher moves from desk to desk checking the progress of the pupils and occasionally he writes spelling words on the blackboard.

This lesson highlights the problem referred to in Chapter 2 concerning the most effective use of scarce staff resources in a school. Here a specialist teacher of modern languages is engaged in a descriptive exercise which makes demands of his enthusiasm, organizational skills, and local knowledge of a particular French situation, but in the lesson he makes very little use of his linguistic expertise.

It is when one encounters lessons of this kind that the problem of selecting significant information to transmit to children becomes clearly evident. Faced with a class of thirty low ability children many teachers seek to introduce a variety of teaching approaches into a single lesson, and over a series of lessons group work, projects, class worksheet exercises, film shows, radio tapes and other activities may be employed. This variety is introduced partly to reduce behavioural problems which may accompany boredom for some pupils, and partly because it permits particular pupils to learn from materials or teaching styles which are more appropriate for them. Sometimes the topic chosen for study and the availability of resources will also produce variety.

But for the inclusion of the information about Italy this lesson would have been more usefully described as a lesson in French Studies. The emphasis upon comparison introduces a more broadly defined European element. The major difficulty for the teacher is defining why he presented the information in the way he did. Is the information interesting for its own sake or does it contribute to a wider understanding of the way of life of the selected nations? In the search for the typical how serious is the danger of stereotyping and how much emphasis is placed upon the oddities in the scene as opposed to the more general characteristics? Can more be gained through the making of comparisons between countries than through the making of contrasts?

This teacher could well be commended for the fact that he chose to show only six slides—he avoided the temptation to show dozens— and it is clear that the slides were carefully chosen to illustrate particular points. The use of a worksheet linked to the slides ensured that the pupils viewed the slides carefully and reinforced their observation. If the pupils had been fortunate enough to be going on a

*Mary Glasgow Publications Ltd.

school study visit to France or Italy then the lesson would have been useful as preparation. Without this possibility then the knowledge acquired in this particular lesson appears to be of passing interest, comparable to the information which pupils pick up from casual reading of magazines or news broadcasts on television.

There is evidence in this lesson for a search for a structure on which to hang the factual data obtained from the slides. Concepts of food supply and retailing are elaborated during the lesson. Pupils are here encouraged to draw comparisons between their local experience in their own community and the foreign experience. It is to be hoped that pupils should be able to generalize from lessons of this kind to explore similar or contrasting phenomena in other European countries as well as in countries on other continents. However, if all that the pupils remember of this lesson is that the French eat horsemeat and Italian children drink wine with their meals then the place of lessons like this in the curricula of schoolchildren is open to question.

Lesson 2   The Energy Crisis: Resource-Based, Individual Enquiry

For the twenty-five traditional sixth formers in this class European Studies is a minority time course of a year's duration at the end of which they will be entered for a CEE examination. In this school all the sixth formers follow the same minority time programme and European Studies was originally introduced to see whether it would capture the interest of the pupils, since several other courses had been heavily criticized for their 'irrelevant content' and 'uninspired and uninspirational teaching'. The examination had been added later as a spur to serious interest and work. The majority of marks in the examination were allocated to course work and the course was designed as a series of autonomous units. For each unit an array of resources had been collected by the two teachers responsible for the course (a geographer and a French specialist) and in the majority of the lessons the pupils read and wrote on topics determined by the teachers.

This lesson, like the previous two lessons in the course, is given over to private study by the pupils and their attention is focused on an essay title, 'How can the Common Market help Britain to solve her energy crisis?' The newness of the energy crisis poses difficulties for those pupils who would prefer to find answers to questions in a single textbook, because, for this topic, textbooks are not available. To help them to answer the question the teacher has provided the last two years' issues of several bank reviews, cuttings from national newspapers, articles from the 'European Studies Teachers' Series', information sheets from oil companies and the National Coal Board, recent issues of *The Economist*, and publications from the European Communities Information Service. These materials are scattered on a table near the centre of the room. The pupils are seated singly or in groups, talking, reading, writing, drawing maps and diagrams. Occasionally, a pupil wanders out of the room to visit the library to check information or to search for more data. The teacher engages in dialogues in response to questions in which explanations are sometimes sought and at other times guidance is required on sources of particular information.

Although homework is not a feature of the course it is clear that some pupils prefer to work at home rather than in class. At the end of the lesson several pupils borrow materials and sign a book recording what they have borrowed. The essays will need to be finished by the following week and the marks awarded for the essays will contribute to the pupils' total in the final CEE assessment.

Unimpaired by the restrictions associated with the requirements of external examinations, the teacher of European Studies either as a minority time course or as a CEE Mode 3 course in the sixth form is free to select topics and explore them at length and in detail. Generally, his pupils will be mature and they will already have been successful in examinations at CSE or GCE levels. They may have passes in modern languages and subjects drawn from the broad field of the humanities and they may be continuing studies in these fields to more advanced levels. They enter the sixth form with knowledge, skills and interests with which it is possible to construct a significant European Studies course.

In any group of sixth formers there will be those who attend minority time courses for no other reason than that it is required of them by the school. If pupils with this attitude are in the majority then it is unlikely that a teacher will be able to sustain a series of lessons of the lecture or chalk-and-talk variety. Fortunately, the problem of suitable teaching resources which preoccupies the teacher of European Studies with younger and less able pupils is far less important for the sixth-form teacher. He can utilize articles from newspapers and journals and a wide array of textual material without having to spend much time explaining and defining their contents. When topics chosen for study are of topical interest then this is an important asset. In the lesson described the teacher, having set the essay title and provided reading materials, is free to adopt the roles of observer and unobtrusive guide referred to in the description of Daffern's course (page 51).

Not only are the pupils able to select the materials they wish to consult they are also free to leave the classroom in order to consult other sources elsewhere in the school. In some schools sixth formers are permitted to leave the school during the school day to visit public libraries and they may also work at home rather than in school. A pupil who takes a serious interest in a particular topic may well dispense with the teacher, choosing to work on a problem in his own way in his own time. It is this emphasis on individual enquiry which is the most striking feature of European Studies courses in the sixth form and the difference between this approach and that described in the first example in this chapter is enormous. It must be emphasized that a minority time course of European Studies may well be a means to an end, the end being the development of individual study skills such as the collection, evaluation and utilization of data to answer essay questions, i.e. the procedural objectives referred to in the first chapter, and the choice of Europe as the substantive area for study may be a secondary consideration. The broad political, cultural, social and vocational aims, also referred to in Chapter 1, are secondary to the specific objectives.

Lesson 3   Petnas: A Simulation Exercise

The class comprises twenty first-year sixth formers. Arriving for their European Studies lesson these 'new' sixth formers find that the classroom furniture has been re-arranged. Instead of the desks and chairs forming a tidy semi-circle around the teacher's desk they have been placed to form a square. On each row of desks there is a card and on each card, written in bold letters, there is a different unfamiliar word—Nortron, Setha, Wesnet and Elney.

The pupils know where to sit for the teacher, a history specialist, had previously arranged the class in four groups and the pupils had been told individually to which groups they had been allocated and simultaneously they had received two information sheets, one which was common to the whole class and the other for particular group members. The common sheet (Fig. 15) describes certain characteristics of an imaginary island named Petnas. It includes a map which shows the location of two provinces and two cities. The provinces are Nortron and Setha and the cities are Elney and Wesnet. Only when all the pupils are seated do they know the membership of the groups.

The teacher explains the procedure for the simulation. In the first ten minutes the group members discuss informally their position concerning the problem stated on the information sheet. At the end of the time each group should have selected a spokesman who would state the case for their area being a suitable location for the university and associated new town. Five minutes would be allowed for each spokesman to state his case. Questions of clarification could be posed by members of other groups within the five minute periods. At the end of the four statements a ten minute period would follow during which time inter-group discussion on a bilateral or multilateral basis could take place. At the end of the forty minute lesson a decision has to be reached as to the area in which the university and new town would be located.

Having outlined the procedure the teacher acts as chairman, keeping a sharp eye on the clock and ensuring that the outlined procedure is followed.

The lesson is the concluding lesson of a series of twelve, spread over six weeks, in a minority time European Studies course. The theme for the six weeks was 'Cultural Minorities in Europe' and the pupils have followed seminars and lectures which have focused on political, economic and social problems in Yugoslavia, France, Spain and Belgium associated with cultural minorities identified principally by language. It is hoped that in the simulation exercise the pupils are recalling the data presented in the previous lessons and applying some of the principles and concepts which they have already discussed.

The pupils appear to experience little difficulty in adopting their roles. Having already received some guidance as to the possible lines their arguments might follow they engage in earnest discussions in which their main task is determining which points should be emphasized by their spokesmen. In these discussions those pupils who are most argumentative and most forceful in debate are elected spokesmen. The spokesmen, in turn, present their arguments bluntly and persuasively and the teacher insists that the time limits are kept. At the conclusion of the individual statements a period of approximately five minutes of cross-group and inter-individual argument and counter-argument breaks out which subsides as it becomes evident that three of the four groups appear to have reached a common understanding. These three groups have agreed to press for the new enterprise to be located in Nortron province, midway between Elney and Wesnet in the foothills of the central mountain range. Setha is isolated. The exercise concludes with three of the groups electing a spokesman who argues a powerful case and the spokesman for Setha makes a final appeal and a restatement of his group's case.

The lesson ends with the teacher calling the class to order and reminding the pupils of the relevance of the exercise to their previous studies. Particular reference is made to the controversy surrounding the position of the University of Louvain (Leuven) in Belgium and the significance of the Belgian language frontier, and also the debate which surrounded the selection of a site for a new Scottish university prior to the decision to found a university at Stirling. The pupils leave the lesson as the bell rings and continue their arguments as they move down the corridor.

Information sheet for Petnas Simulation

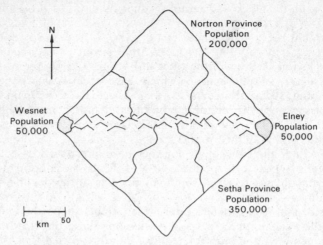

Fig. 15.

The Nortron people invaded this island in 960 A.D. and settled in the area north of the mountains. Their religion, Murman, is different from that of the Sethars who live in the south and hold the Tai faith.

In 1780 the island was united to form one nation governed from the capital city Wesnet.

The two provinces depend on mixed farming and they are both prosperous. The rivers provide good drainage and irrigation, and the climate is cool temperate. Culturally the areas are differentiated by religion and language. Good road and rail links follow the coastlines and unite the two provinces. Each province has its own radio and television services.

Elney is the only commercial port and the industrial centre serving both provinces. It derives hydro-electric power for the industries from mountain streams on the northern side of the mountain range. Both languages, Nortron and Sethar, are used in the city.

Wesnet is the seat of the federal government and government business is conducted in both languages. Neither province has been able to dominate national affairs for both cities and provinces share in a delicate balance of power.

The Minister of Education has secured finance for the foundation of the nation's first university. A meeting has been called to discuss the siting of this university and representatives have come from Wesnet and Elney and from the two provinces. The proposed development will incorporate a university and an associated new town housing eventually a population of 15,000.

Group Information Sheets for Petnas Simulation

WESNET—the administrative capital
Your overall policy is to minimize provincial jealousy and to maintain political stability. You may feel that a compromise on your desire for the project will be necessary. However Wesnet can offer:
  (a) the existing cultural and professional life of a bilingual capital city;
  (b) expanding job opportunities in the civil service;
  (c) proximity to government for government research contracts;
  (d) 'a neutral base' since the capital is already bilingual;
  (e) a convenient location midway between the two provinces so that students from both provinces will have no difficulty travelling to and from it.

ELNEY—the commercial centre
You depend on trade with the whole of the country and you are principally concerned with sustaining your markets and obtaining food supplies and raw materials from the two provinces. However Elney can offer:
  (a) expanding job opportunities in the commercial and industrial enterprises;
  (b) proximity to economically useful research projects;
  (c) good communications between the two provinces;
  (d) a culturally impoverished environment which would benefit enormously from a university and all the facilities associated with it;
  (e) 'a neutral base' since the city is already bilingual.

NORTRON—the northern province
The population of this province is less than that of Setha and the citizens are regarded as culturally inferior principally because they arrived later on the island.
Siting the university in Nortron would:
  (a) act as a boost for Nortron language and culture;
  (b) provide an accessible centre for students from both the big cities;
  (c) encourage the location of other cultural facilities;
  (d) promote decentralization, away from the major urban centres of wealth and population;
  (e) encourage diversification in the provincial economy which may suffer from over-dependence on farming.

SETHA—the southern province
Many residents of Setha regard the citizens of Nortron as newcomers
and second class citizens. They regard a university as theirs by right.
Siting the university in Setha would:
  (a) be a recognition of Setha's cultural superiority;
  (b) provide an accessible centre for students from both the big cities;
  (c) encourage the location of other cultural facilities;
  (d) promote decentralization away from the major urban centres of
       wealth and population;
  (e) encourage diversification in the provincial economy which may
       suffer from over-dependence on farming.

This lesson provides some striking contrasts with the first lesson
described earlier in the chapter. The most significant difference is to be
seen in the different roles of teachers and pupils in the two situations.
In the first lesson the teacher is the supplier of information, he has not
only decided on the topic to be taught but also he is in complete control
of the sequence of stages through which the lesson proceeds. He guides
the pupils in the way he wants them to learn what he considers
important; they view particular aspects of each slide and answer
questions where the answers are predictable ('closed' questions in the
language of classroom interaction studies). The decision to employ such
tightly controlled techniques of teaching may well be determined by
reasons of social control—a freer situation may be exploited by pupils
and render teaching difficult if not impossible. With more highly
motivated sixth formers, pupils who are defined by the fact that they
have decided to stay in school beyond the leaving age of 16, the problem
of social control, though not the problems associated with motivation,
are largely removed. At the end of a series of lessons, which could well
have been of an instructional kind similar to the other lesson described,
a simulation serves not only to bring a unit of work, or a topic, to an
interesting end it also serves to motivate the pupils towards the next
topic to be taken up in the succeeding lessons. It is the openness of the
simulation which distinguishes it so clearly from the instructional
lesson.

In procedural terms, the objective behind this lesson may have been
the involvement or the participation of pupils in an interesting
problem-solving exercise in which the factual knowledge and skills
necessary to solve the problem (see Chapter 4) have already been
acquired in the preceding lessons. The teacher, apparently reduced to a
timekeeper although he has in fact spent some considerable time
planning the simulation long before the lesson, plays an important role
in the exercise. By carefully observing the pupils, individually and in
their groups, he is able to evaluate what they have learned and also how

effective his teaching through the topic has been. On the basis of these observations he can modify his teaching in future years and also consider ways by which he can help individuals who have demonstrated certain weaknesses during the simulation.

Discussion with the teachers concerned could reveal that their aims and objectives with the two classes were identical. The methods used to achieve them are clearly quite different. At the end of the lessons the teacher of the first lesson will, by marking the work sheets know quite clearly how much his pupils have learned in terms of what he wanted them to learn. In the simulation the teacher is left with a different sort of assessment. Assessing what pupils have learned in any school course is a vitally important part of teaching. It is to this aspect which we turn in the next chapter.

CHAPTER EIGHT

Examining European Studies

The establishment of new regional examination boards for Certificate of Secondary Education (CSE) examinations generated a new drive to design courses for the sixteen-year-old school leaver. In this chapter I shall outline the procedures necessary for a European Studies course to be approved by a CSE board and then discuss testing techniques currently being employed in European Studies examinations.

The Certificate of Secondary Education
Until 1966 a school pupil of sixteen wishing to hold nationally accepted school-leaving qualifications in England and Wales would have been entered in one or more subjects for General Certificate of Education (GCE) examinations at Ordinary level. These were conducted by regional examination boards and they were taken by pupils of above average ability. These examinations were not designed for the great majority of sixteen-year-olds and most of the non-examination pupils left secondary school at the age of fifteen. Examinations did exist for the less able youngsters, sometimes organized on a local basis, e.g. the Reading Schools Leaving Certificate and the ULCI examinations, and sometimes on a national basis, e.g. City and Guilds examinations and RSA examinations. These and other arrangements were the subject of the Beloe Report (HMSO 1960) and the Fourth Report of the Secondary Schools Examinations Council (1961). The main conclusion of the Beloe Report was that 'the time had come for the Minister to encourage by his recognition schemes of regional examinations on a subject basis, largely and effectively under the control of teachers, co-ordinated by a central body with the help of a research and development unit, and aimed at a level somewhat below that of the GCE Ordinary level for pupils completing a five year secondary school course'.

These proposals were accepted and fifteen regional examination boards co-ordinated by the Schools Council were established. Every board appointed subject panels of teachers to draft syllabuses and specimen examination papers and the first candidates were entered for CSE examinations in 1966.

The regional boards permit candidates to be examined in any subject under three different types of arrangements referred to as modes. In Mode 1 the syllabus and related examination procedures are designed by the subject panel of the board and the pupils' work is examined externally by examiners appointed by the board. In Mode 2 a syllabus is designed by a single school or by a group of schools and if it is approved by the board the pupils are examined by external examinations set and marked by the board. In Mode 3 a single school designs its own syllabus which is submitted to the board for approval, examination procedures are also designed within the school and moderated by the board, the candidates' work is examined internally by the school and the final marks are moderated by an external examiner, or moderator, appointed by the board.

Irrespective of the mode employed candidates are finally allocated a CSE grade on a five point numerical scale on which Grade 1 is defined as being equivalent to a GCE 'O' level pass in the subject, and Grade 4 is a pass at the level of attainment considered average for the whole age group.

'Mode 3 is fairly uncommon in comparison with Mode 1; entries under Mode 3 are less than one-fifth of those under Mode 1 over the country as a whole' (Hoste and Bloomfield 1975). For European Studies however Mode 3 is the rule rather than the exception. The first CSE candidates to be examined in a course labelled 'European Studies' were from the St Richard of Chichester School in London. The course was approved by the Metropolitan Regional Examinations Board as a Mode 3 course and the first examination was conducted in 1968 (O'Connell 1968). Since then many more Mode 3 CSE European Studies courses have been approved in many regions. As an indication of the growth in numbers there was a single European Studies course in the North West in 1970 and by 1976 fourteen courses had been approved for CSE Mode 3 examination.

Mode 3 CSE Course Approval
Each board has developed its own distinctive procedure for approving European Studies courses. Basically, a European Studies teacher or team of teachers must provide the board with a detailed statement of course aims and objectives, a synopsis of course content and a clear description of examination proposals together with a precise account of how marks will be allocated.

Brief descriptions of two moderating procedures serve to illustrate the differences in practice within boards.

The first example is based upon the procedures employed* by the North West Regional Examinations Board to consider Mode 3 European Studies courses.

The teacher who intends to submit a course proposal has almost certainly read a booklet published by the board which gives guidance to teachers preparing CSE Mode 3 course proposals (North West Regional Examinations Board 1976). Having submitted a course proposal the teacher is visited by a moderator appointed by the board and together they discuss the proposal. Suggestions may be made by the moderator for minor amendments or major modifications to the proposal. The teacher considers such suggestions and a new proposal may be submitted to the moderator for him to decide whether to recommend to the board approval or rejection of the course. The moderator prepares a report which is considered by the chief moderator for European Studies before it is discussed by a curriculum sub-committee. Assuming that this sub-committee accepts the moderators' recommendations for approval the school is informed that the course has been approved for examination by the board. Pupils may then be entered for examinations. In the winter term prior to the summer examination the school submits an examination paper for moderation and when the moderator agrees that the examination paper is satisfactory the paper is prepared for the pupils. After the examinations have been taken the moderator visits the school to moderate the marks and he then recommends to the board a list of pupils with grades based upon the marks. The moderator finally writes a report on the examinations which is read by the chief moderator before it is formally submitted to the board. A copy of this report is sent to the school.

This procedure can be summarized in a simple flow diagram (Fig. 16).

This moderation procedure is sometimes referred to as a single-stage procedure and is simpler than the multi-stage procedure employed by some other boards. Using a multi-stage procedure the boards have tried to ensure that there is close local involvement of teachers in the design and moderation of courses and that there is a standardisation of marks and grades between schools and groups of schools within the region administered by a particular board. In the Southern Regional Examination Board schools are paired for this, while in the West Yorkshire and Lindsey Regional Examinations Board schools are grouped into consortia. The multi-stage procedure is summarized in Fig. 17.

Teachers of European Studies encounter considerable difficulty in

*It must be emphasized that these procedures are regularly reviewed and while they were accurate in 1977 they are liable to change.

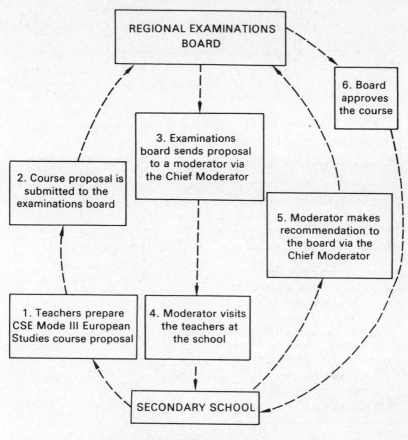

REGIONAL EXAMINATIONS
BOARD

6. Board
approves
the course

3. Examinations
board sends proposal
to a moderator via
the Chief Moderator

2. Course proposal is
submitted to the
examinations board

5. Moderator makes
recommendation to
the board via the
Chief Moderator

1. Teachers prepare
CSE Mode III European
Studies course proposal

4. Moderator visits
the teachers at
the school

SECONDARY SCHOOL

Fig. 16

constructing Mode 3 courses for two main reasons: first, until recently there have been no GCE 'O' level or CSE Mode 1 models of European Studies syllabuses and examination papers on which to construct a Mode 3 course (where GCE and Mode 1 courses exist they have followed Mode 3 CSE practice); second, existing Mode 3 courses are so tied to particular schools that it is difficult for a teacher to apply them to his own situation. When boards have attempted to define criteria for European Studies courses they have produced general statements which give little useful guidance except in providing teachers with considerable freedom to initiate new course arrangements.

Thorne (1975) has provided a summary of the criteria used for European Studies assessment in the Southern Regional Examinations

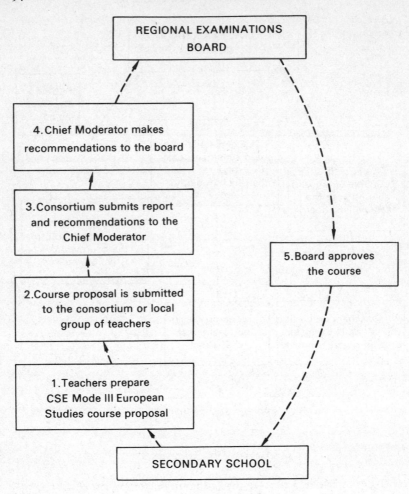

Fig. 17

Board: '—That the pupil has a certain amount of background knowledge of the countries of Europe based on reading, observation, recording and comprehension, and will therefore be able to recall facts in some or all of the following sections: (a) simple language usage; (b) simple linguistic development; (c) economic life; (d) social life and customs.

'—That the pupil has some understanding of how and why Europe has arrived at its present state and the ability to explain how and why some of the present situations have arisen.

'—That the pupil can recognize a problem, can analyse a situation and is capable of some evaluation of the possible solutions.'

In the North West Regional Examinations Board three criteria are used to guide teachers in drafting European Studies syllabuses:

1 syllabuses must be inter-disciplinary because if the courses were uni-disciplinary they would bear the title of the discipline on which they were based;

2 syllabuses bearing the title 'European Studies' must be pan-European in the extent of the studies because syllabuses focusing on a single nation would be more accurately titled French Studies or German Studies, etc.;

3 syllabuses should be contemporary in emphasis, contemporary being defined as post-1945 although this does not exclude pre-1945 historical studies.

Not surprisingly, with such loose criteria, Mode 3 courses in European Studies, even within single boards, display a wide variety of objectives, syllabus content and modes of assessment.

The Role of the Moderator

A Mode 3 moderator, usually a schoolteacher, receives from a board a school's proposal for a European Studies course. Usually this proposal will be written on a form provided by the board. In the North West Regional Examinations Board the form contains these questions:

NORTH WEST REGIONAL EXAMINATIONS BOARD
Certificate of Secondary Education
MODE 3: PROPOSAL

This proposal must be submitted in accordance with the Board's current regulations set out in Pamphlet No. 2 'Mode 3. Regulations and Notes for Guidance' March 1976. The Headteacher/Principal of every registered centre has been provided with this pamphlet.

1. Title of subject (for entry on the certificate)

....

2. Full name and address of centre

....

....

....

Centre Number.......................... Telephone number...................

Name of Headteacher/Principal making the proposal

....

3. In which year will awards be sought under this proposal for the first time? (see regulation 10.3)

    19.....

4. Does the Board provide an examination under Mode 1 in the same subject or in a related subject?   YES ☐   NO ☐
    (see regulations 10.4 and 10.5)

    If the answer is 'yes' in what way does your proposal differ in content of syllabus or form of examination from the Board's provision under Mode 1?

    ....

    ....

    ....

5. Does the content of the proposed syllabus overlap any other CSE syllabus under Mode 2 or Mode 3 on which candidates are examined   YES ☐   NO ☐
    at your centre?
    (see regulations 10.4 and 10.5)

    If the answer is 'yes' please give brief details.

    ....

    ....

    ....

6. Please indicate in the spaces below the forms of examination to be used (see regulation 10.6)

Forms of examination to be used	General description	% of total mark	Abilities and/or skills for which marks will be awarded

Signed ....
                                                    (Headteacher/Principal)

Fig. 18. Proposal form for Mode 3 CSE European Studies

NORTH WEST REGIONAL EXAMINATIONS BOARD
Certificate of Secondary Education

SPECIFICATION OF END-OF-COURSE TEST

Two copies of this form must be attached to the front of any specimen test that constitutes part of a Mode 3 proposal.

Full name and address of centre

Centre number

Title (for entry on the certificate)

Form of test (e.g. written, practical, aural, oral)

Paper number (if appropriate)   1   2   3   4

Title of each section	Number of questions in each section	Types of questions	Number to be attempted by candidate	Place for candidate's responses

Do you intend to use this specimen test as an actual test in the first year of the examination?

YES ☐   NO ☐

Signed.. Date...............................
Headteacher/Principal

Fig. 19. Specification sheet: end-of-course test

Having read a course proposal the moderator checks the responses to the questions against the practices laid down by the board and any criteria defined by the board for the particular subject or course. He notes any unclear or ambiguous points and any statements of content which he considers require more or less emphasis. He will consider carefully the proposed mode of assessment and the balance in the allocation of marks.

He arranges a visit to the school to meet the teacher or team of teachers responsible for the course and at this meeting any vagueness or ambiguity is clarified, suggestions for improving the course proposal are made, and the moderator is then able to complete the report form which he must return to the board. The NWREB form is reproduced as Fig. 20.

NORTH WEST REGIONAL EXAMINATIONS BOARD
Certificate of Secondary Education

First report on Mode 3 proposal—Reference number..........................

Title of subject (for entry on the certificate).....................................

Full name and address of centre...

....

PLEASE ANSWER EVERY QUESTION YES OR NO BY CIRCLING THE APPROPRIATE RESPONSE

1. Does the title reflect accurately the contents of the syllabus? YES NO

2. Is the breadth and depth of the syllabus appropriate to the award of a FULL range of grades? YES NO

3. Are the resources for its teaching available? YES NO

4. Do the component parts of the examination provide for a proper examination of the candidates' abilities and/or skills? YES NO

5. Are these abilities and/or skills clearly described so as to enable a moderator, at the completion of the course, to judge the achievement of each candidate? YES NO

6. (a) Does the content of the syllabus overlap any other CSE syllabus under Modes 1, 2 and 3 on which candidates are examined at this centre? YES NO

    (b) If the answer to (a) is 'yes', name any syllabus with which the overlap appears sufficient to justify prohibition by the Board of entry to examination on more than one of these syllabuses in any one year.

    ....

7. Is each component of the examination given a
    minimum weighting of 20%?   YES   NO
8. If end-of-course tests, e.g. written, practical,
    aural, oral, are to be used does each specimen
    test include:
    (a) a clear specification?   YES   NO
    (b) adequate specimen answers?   YES   NO
    (c) a clear marking scheme?   YES   NO

9. Is the standard of each test appropriate to the
    award of a FULL range of grades?   YES   NO
10. Is each test well constructed?   YES   NO

11. Have you reached agreement with the centre on
    the scope of the evidence that will be offered to
    you in support of the marks awarded?   YES   NO

Moderator's comments

I recommend/do not recommend this proposal for acceptance by the
Board. (Please delete as appropriate)

....
(Moderator)

Note that the date for the first examination will be fixed by the
Examinations Committee and that a moderator has no authority to
'give approval' to any arrangement that does not conform to the
Board's regulations.

_____

Chief moderator's comments

I recommend/do not recommend this proposal for acceptance by the
Board. (Please delete as appropriate)

....
(Chief moderator)

Fig. 20. CSE Mode 3 proposal report form

The moderator must recommend to the board the acceptance or rejection of the proposed courses. If the board decides to accept a course then the moderator's next task will be the acceptance of the school's examination papers if end-of-course examination papers are included in the formal assessment. Most Mode 3 European Studies examinations incorporate such papers. He will also examine any course work or project work of a sample or of all the candidates. Depending on the practice of the board there may be some inter-school moderation of marks and grades. The moderator finally recommends the grades for the candidates to the board.

CSE European Studies Examinations

All formal examinations must be valid, reliable and produce results which are comparable between schools. An examination is valid if it measures what it is designed to measure. If an examination produces consistent results then it is reliable. In CSE examinations where grades are awarded by a regional examinations board the results obtainable in any one school must be comparable with results obtainable in other schools examining candidates in the same subject.

Fig. 21 summarizes the methods of examining employed by teachers of nine European Studies courses approved by the North West Regional Examinations Board. Broadly, these methods can be grouped under four headings: written examinations, oral examinations, course work and projects.

1　Written Examinations

Written examinations in European Studies owe much in their construction to the style and techniques employed in other subjects, especially to geography, history and modern languages. Generally the examinations incorporate a mixture of objective questions and subjective questions. The balance between objective and subjective questions and the actual type of questions incorporated into the paper are determined by the objectives set for the course and the relative emphases given to the various course objectives.

Before constructing a written examination paper a teacher is well advised to list the instructional objectives he wishes to examine and then to classify these and allocate marks to the classes so obtained. (See Gronlund 1970, Lawton and Dufour 1974 and Schools Council Examinations Bulletin 32, 1975c for examples.) Objectives which the candidates *must* attain should be placed in a compulsory section of the examination paper and those where some choice is permitted can be placed in a section of questions from which the candidate may select a specified number of questions to answer. The number of abilities which must be tested will determine how many question papers are required,

School	METHODS OF EXAMINING								Subject of Initiating Teacher
	Written Exam (Non-Foreign Language)	Written Exam (Foreign Language)	Oral Exam (Non-Foreign Language)	Oral Exam (Foreign Language)	Aural Exam (Foreign Language)	Course work	Single Projects	More than one Project	
A	40	*	*	*	*	30	*	30	Modern Languages
B	50	20	*	10	*	*	20	*	Modern Languages
C	50	*	*	*	*	25	25	*	Modern Languages
D	50	*	*	15	*	10	25	*	History
E	70	*	5	*	*	15	10	*	History
F	48	*	*	*	*	40	12	*	English
G	30	20	*	10	5	5	*	30	Modern Languages
H	50	*	*	*	*	*	*	50	Modern Languages
I	20	*	10	*	*	20	50	*	History

Fig. 21. Methods of Examining Employed in Nine CSE Mode 3 European Studies Courses

(Figures show percentage of marks allocated to each method. It should be noted that a 1976 regulation of the board requires that each form of examination must account for at least 20% of the final mark.)

how many sections and questions are included in each paper and the length of time required for each paper. The style of questions to be used will determine whether the pupils require specially prepared answer books or simply sheets of paper on which to write their answers.

I have already referred to the division between subjective and objective questions. Subjective questions are those which are answered in continuous prose, usually essays. Objective questions are designed to present pupils with precise problems where the solution is pre-determined. Subjective questions are open-ended, providing scope for a free response from the candidate, while objective questions can be answered only by a restricted response.

Essay Questions
Few teachers experience difficulty in framing essay questions. Essay titles may appear with a brief quotation on which the pupils are asked to comment or the pupils may be asked to discuss the quotation in the light of some other evidence with which they are expected to be familiar. Titles may also appear as invitations to 'describe', 'examine', 'give reasons for', 'outline', 'describe', 'compare and contrast', 'summarize'. Although it is relatively easy to construct suitable titles the resulting essays are extremely difficult to mark. The requests made by examination boards for mark schemes or specimen answers are an attempt to reduce subjective, impressionistic and inconsistent marking, but the very existence of a mark scheme can serve to make essay questions objective in character and reduce their value as open exercises within an examination. If essays are marked on a tight, objective mark scheme then there is a strong case for substituting objective questions for essay questions.

Yet devising the mark scheme forces the examiner to anticipate the candidates' likely responses and the very exercise of thinking through the answers is likely to lead him to improve the quality of the questions themselves. The gains in consistency and in marking time will also be considerable.

Reading through many CSE European Studies examination papers I am struck by the assumption, inherent in the choice offered to candidates, that all questions set are equally difficult. It is obvious that if only one 'compare and contrast' question is set on a paper where a choice of essays is available all the candidates may decide not to attempt that question. The teacher is then left at the end of a course without knowing if his pupils are capable, under examination conditions, of writing intelligently about comparisons and contrasts. The abilities to 'describe' or 'give reasons' are different from the ability to 'compare and contrast' and the latter may be a higher order intellectual activity than the other two. In which case, if it is the teacher's intention to test this higher order ability for *all* the pupils then there is obviously a case for making such essays compulsory, or at least some essay *types*, so that the pupils are tested in important abilities.

It is in the control of essay marking that a moderator plays an important role. It has been my experience as a moderator to request the remarking of batches of essays where teachers have added marks for essays in a CSE examination on the basis of the pupils' behaviour and academic records during a course. As one teacher commented in response to a query why a particular candidate had acquired five 'extra marks' in an essay, 'Well, he's a hard worker and he's the most co-operative boy in the class'. In the same way, marks are sometimes removed quite arbitrarily for poor spelling, bad grammar or untidy handwriting. A clear mark scheme protects the pupil and the teacher from these tendencies.

Increasingly CSE essay questions include instructions for the candidate concerning the number of words to which the answer should be restricted and guidance for the candidate on the way in which marks are distributed when a question is divided into sub-parts. Some schools permit candidates in European Studies examinations to use atlases when answering essay questions.

These six essay titles are good examples of the questions commonly posed in CSE European Studies examinations.

1 Regional development is an important part of the EEC's plans. Choose one European country with contrasting rich and poor regions. Explain why this situation has developed and outline plans made to improve the poorer regions.

2 Describe some of the main urban problems in Moscow *or* Stockholm *or* Paris in the post-1945 period, and some of the attempts made to solve them. How far have the attempts been successful?

3 Outline the political organization of the EEC with particular reference to the relationships between the Council of Ministers, the European Parliament, the Commission and the Court of Justice.

4 Discuss the causes and the effects of ONE of the following:
   (a) the building of the Berlin Wall,
   (b) the Hungarian uprising,
   (c) the Czech uprising,
   (d) the Paris May Riots.

5 Compare and contrast the educational systems of France and Poland with special reference to either primary education or secondary education.

6   Choose one of the following political leaders, outline his life story and assess his importance in post-war Europe:
   (a) de Gaulle,
   (b) Churchill,
   (c) Spaak,
   (d) Stalin,
   (e) Franco.

Objective Questions

Since European Studies courses are distinguished principally by the fact that they focus on a continent we should expect pupils who have studied aspects of Europe to have a distinctive factual store of knowledge about Europe. To ensure that these facts have been remembered the objective test can be readily employed. While not simply restricted to testing straightforward recall of facts it is to do this that objective tests are most widely used.

A simple classification of techniques of objective testing would be multiple choice questions, true-false questions, and matching questions.

Multiple Choice Questions

Structurally a multiple choice question is composed of three parts the stem, foils (or distractors) and a keyed response (the correct answer). In a useful analysis of objective test items Berg (1965) distinguishes between items based on the recognition of:
   1 memorized content details; 2 specific factual information; 3 concepts;
and 'items which require thought and understanding through:
   1 the translation of knowledge into other terms; 2 the use of knowledge in problem-solving situations; 3 the ability to interpret social studies data'.

This classification highlights the scope for testing afforded by multiple choice questions since all these items are capable of translation into such questions. On one end of the scale questions may serve as simple stimuli or cues to which the pupil responds with an answer which has been memorized while at the other end of the scale the pupil is required to think carefully through a problem or apply his knowledge to a new situation or to new data. These questions illustrate this range.

1   Compulsory education begins in France for children when they are
   (a) 5 years old,   (c) 3 years old,
   (b) 6 years old,   (d) 4 years old.

2 The Mansholt Plan dealt with
   (a) regional development,
   (b) aid to underdeveloped countries,
   (c) agriculture
   (d) tariffs.
3 Flats are a feature of urban life in Sweden because
   (a) the Swedes prefer to live in small flats rather than in large houses,
   (b) the Swedes have few children and therefore do not need houses,
   (c) the average Swede cannot afford the high cost of a house,
   (d) there is a shortage of building land.
4 CELIB is an organization which has been working
   (a) to promote the interests of Brittany,
   (b) to promote tourism in Languedoc,
   (c) to provide housing for the poorer sections of the community,
   (d) to improve private education.
5 *Migrant Workers Employed in the European Community*

Country of Origin	Country of Employment			European Community (total 1973)
	France (December 1976)	Germany (January 1973)	Italy (average 1971)	
Algeria	450,000	2,000	0	456,000
Belgium	25,000	11,000	539	74,000
Denmark	1,000	4,000	248	7,500
France		51,000	4,145	93,000
Germany	25,000		7,190	81,000
Greece	5,000	268,096	768	332,000
Ireland	1,000	0	300	471,000
Italy	230,000	409,689		858,000
Luxembourg	2,000	1,450	32	5,400
Morocco	120,000	15,317	0	168,000
Netherlands	5,000	70,000	1,146	92,000
Portugal	380,000	69,099	631	469,000
Spain	270,000	179,498	2,006	527,000
Tunisia	60,000	11,162	0	74,000
Turkey	18,000	528,239	317	582,000
United Kingdom	10,000	19,000	4,500	46,000
Yugoslavia	50,000	466,128	4,103	535,000

This table shows that the member of the European Communities supplying most immigrant workers to France and Germany is
(a) Turkey,
(b) Spain,
(c) Italy,
(d) Netherlands,
(e) Another (specify)......................................

The principal problem of multiple choice questions is the triviality of much of the information which the pupil is asked to recall. Determining precisely which facts are worth remembering is clearly a problem for the individual teacher because only he knows the emphases in his teaching which will be directly related to his course objectives. It is difficult to see why pupils should be expected to remember the colours of national flags, the eating habits and foods of foreign countries, the registration plates of cars and the names of assorted novelists, artists, newspapers, capital cities, railway stations and sporting heroes which crop up so regularly in CSE European Studies examination papers.

Multiple choice questions must obviously be constructed carefully to avoid ambiguity, to reduce guesswork on the part of the candidate, and to produce sensible foils. There is a serious temptation to introduce silly foils and these do not contribute to the item as a testing instrument. Undoubtedly the attraction of multiple choice questions, as with all objective questions, is the speed and efficiency of the marking coupled with the fact that numerous questions can be attempted by the candidates in a relatively short period of time.

While many of the multiple choice questions employed in European Studies examinations are of the type exemplified in the first two examples above some of the more enterprising teachers have linked the multiple choice technique to statistical tables (as in example 5), photographs, newspaper cartoons, maps, paragraphs of text and other information. Here the questions may still involve a certain amount of information recall but the emphasis in the questions may be more upon the interpretation and analysis of the given information than upon memorization.

What is evident from examination papers and mark schemes in European Studies is that teachers do not distinguish in their allocation of marks between objective questions of differing difficulty. The tendency to give all multiple choice questions a single mark is common and yet there are important distinctions to be made between the trivial and the important in terms of both the information and skills being tested and in the intellectual activity to be tested by the questions.

True-false Questions
Of the true-false question Marshall and Hales (1971) have written 'the true-false item is adaptable for use in situations where the measurement of the acquisition of factual, noninterpretative information is desired—for example, vocabulary, technical terms, formulae, dates and proper names. A comprehensive sampling of content corresponding to such instructional objectives may be rapidly obtained with the true-false test'.

Using the table reproduced on page 105 these items can be written to show the different styles of true-false items.

A   The following is a true-false statement. If you think the statement is true write T on the dotted line preceding the question number. If you think the statement is false write F on the dotted line.

...... 1 There are more migrant workers from Turkey employed in France and Germany than from any other country.

...... 2 The movement of migrant workers is mainly from north Africa to northern Europe.

B   Read the following statements carefully. Decide whether each one is true or false and then circle the letter T (for true) or F (for false) at the end of each statement.

1   There are more migrant workers from Turkey employed in France and Germany than from any other country.   T.   F.

2   The movement of migrant workers is mainly from north Africa to northern Europe.   T.   F.

C   Read the following statements carefully. Decide whether each one is true or false and then write the word TRUE or FALSE on the dotted line at the end of each statement. Then on the line underneath each statement give your reason for your decision.

1   There are more migrant workers from Turkey employed in France and Germany than from any other country. ....

Reason: ....

2   The movement of migrant workers is mainly from north Africa to northern Europe.   ....

Reason: ....

D   Read the following statements carefully. Place a tick in the appropriate box at the end of the statement.

1   There are more children of Italian migrant workers in German schools than in French schools.

True   □

False   □

Not enough information   □

2   In 1970 there were more Turks than Yugoslavs employed in the European Community.

True   □

False   □

Not enough information   □

This testing technique is rarely used in European Studies examination papers. For some teachers the element of guesswork inherent in true-false questions is too dominant and while guesswork is also a feature of multiple choice questions teachers seem to prefer them.

Matching Questions
Matching questions are another way of testing pupils' factual knowledge. Generally they are designed to elicit the recall of basic pieces of knowledge in a disorganized sort of way. In European Studies examination papers it is not uncommon to find questions of this type:

1   Paris is to France as .... is to Italy.
2   Brussels is to the EEC as .... is to the Council of Europe.
3   The following lists are not in order. Copy the left hand list and change the order of the right hand list to show which item belongs to which:

   (i) (a) Steppes   Switzerland
        (b) Alps   Netherlands
        (c) Fjords   Russia
        (d) Polders   Norway
  (ii) (a) Volkswagen   Gothenburg
        (b) Renault   Eindhoven
        (c) Daf   Paris
        (d) Volvo   Wolfsburg

4   This time-line is divided into five-year periods lettered A to F:

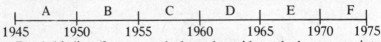

A	B	C	D	E	F
1945	1950	1955	1960	1965	1970	1975

Read this list of events and place alongside each the appropriate letter indicating in which period the event occurred:
(a) the setting up of the EEC ....
(b) the building of the Berlin Wall ....
(c) the Munich Olympic Games ....
(d) the Hungarian uprising ....
(e) the death of General de Gaulle ....

5   In each of the following lists one item is different from the others. Underline the item that is different and then on the line beneath each list state the reason why it is different:
(a) Norway, Denmark, Sweden, Finland.
    Reason ....
(b) Antwerp, Rotterdam, Amsterdam, Brussels.
    Reason ....
(c) Berlin, Paris, Istanbul, Rome.
    Reason ....

(d) Kiel Canal, Manchester Ship Canal, Suez Canal, Gota Canal.
   Reason ....

(e) Alitalia, Lufthansa, SNCF, KLM.
   Reason ....

Variations on these types of items are familiar to geographers who are accustomed to utilizing maps and photographs to match data, e.g. grid references and symbols on Ordnance Survey maps, or place names and locations on foreign maps, and to historians who use extracts from historical documents or contemporary newspaper cartoons as the data to be matched with other information supplied in questions.

Whatever methods of objective testing are employed there are several key rules which the examining teacher needs to keep in the forefront when preparing question papers:

1 Be sure that the testing is congruent with the objectives established for the course.
2 Distinguish carefully between trivia and important information in the substance of the questions.
3 Aim to be comprehensive in the range of knowledge and/or skills to be tested.
4 Give careful consideration to the number of different types of objective questions that can be set and the number of examples of each type to be used.
5 Pay particular attention to the distinction between compulsory questions and optional questions, and to compulsory and optional sections within an examination paper.
6 Allocate marks carefully according to the difficulty of the questions.
7 Be clear, concise and unambiguous in the instructions given to the candidate and in the statements of items.
8 Arrange the questions on the examination paper in such a way that the answers can be easily and speedily marked.
9 Proof read the question paper carefully to eliminate grammatical errors.

Projects

From the very beginning the project has been an integral part of CSE examinations in such subjects as history and geography. Projects are justified by moderators (Hoste and Bloomfield 1975) on the grounds that they provide an opportunity for individuals to select a topic for detailed study.

'Projects (a) allow pupils the chance to seek out information for themselves and use initiative in learning; (b) require pupils to maintain their learning effort over an extended period; (c) give the opportunity for information to be used rather than accumulated; (d) make provision for pupils to comment critically and to pass judgement on information gathered; (e) allow the pupil to consider the situation from several points of view; (f) encourage the gathering and use of different kinds of evidence; (g) permit the display of originality and descriptive ability; (h) encourage the exercise of quality of thinking and reasoning power; (i) make pupils organize information into a coherent comment.' (Hoste and Bloomfield 1975).

As Fig. 21 shows, all the schools examining European Studies through the North West Regional Examinations Board incorporated a project or several projects in their examination arrangements and the mark allocations varied from 10% to 50% of the total marks.

The particular value of the projects in European Studies courses lies in the potential they offer for pupils to engage in thorough studies of aspects of the European scene. For pupils who are fortunate enough to visit a mainland European country during the course of their studies there is the opportunity to write a detailed account of a selected topic and even for the less fortunate pupils purposeful and worthwhile studies may be made based upon pen-pal contacts, school exchange arrangements as well as the more conventional studies from secondary sources.

As a CSE moderator I have been fortunate to read a small number of detailed case studies derived from the first-hand experience of candidates in visits to such countries as Yugoslavia, France and Germany. Such studies are the exception rather than the rule. Indeed in some schools there is an increasing tendency for pupils to fail to submit examinable projects. This is a reflection on the sheer inability of some candidates to prepare projects for several CSE subjects in a short period of time. There are obviously candidates entered for CSE examinations who do not wish to be examined in the courses and these simply absent themselves from essential parts of the examination. Teachers may also treat the project as an autonomous, independent study by the candidate and exercise little control over the candidate's progress in completing the project.

Even when candidates complete the projects it is obvious in European Studies that there is considerable variation in the quality of work produced and in the topics chosen for study. The topics chosen are strongly influenced by the study materials available within a school. Ease of access to tourist literature has produced a glut of projects titled 'Tourism in ....', or 'International Horse Jumping in ....', or 'National Foods of ....' and these projects are colourfully, and frequently irrelevantly, illustrated with the written matter being little more than poorly spelled, ungrammatical dilutions of the sparse information common to tourist brochures. Even when pupils have access to books and encyclopaedias the temptation to copy is strong and there is evidence of the pupils' inability to assess, and up-date, the information they so laboriously accumulate.

Examination boards usually request the schools to state how marks will be allocated within an examinable project. This is a typical scheme:

Observation and accurate recording of information	30%
Relevance of information presented	15%
Originality of written work and illustrations	15%
Conclusions: the application of skills and information	30%
Presentation	10%
	100%

To discourage pupils from including all the information and illustrations they can find on a topic teachers can advise the pupils to frame their project titles as questions to be answered or as hypotheses to be tested. Even a project like 'Tourism in Switzerland' is likely to be much improved if the title is framed in such terms as

'Switzerland's winter season offers a foreign tourist a greater variety of recreational and sporting activities than the summer season.' Discuss.
'What is the relationship between Switzerland's physical features and her tourist industry?'

Not only would titles framed as problems to be solved help the candidates to select, interpret and assess their information, they would also provide examination markers with a more objective form of assessment. When faced by a wide variety of titles it is difficult for an examiner to compare one project with another. The teacher, familiar with the problems encountered in gathering relevant information for particular projects, may well make allowances in his marking for this and he may also reduce, almost subconsciously, the marks of candidates who because of favourable home circumstances have access to rich stores of useful information. Related to this is the difficulty of determining just how much of a pupil's work is in fact his own. All of these factors pose problems for the internal examiner in a school and for the board's moderator who may be seeking a comparison between the assessments of projects in several different schools.

As an attempt to improve the marking of projects some schools have introduced oral examinations and others have included a compulsory question on the subject of the project in the terminal formal examination.

Oral Examinations
In a European Studies context there are two kinds of oral examination. First, foreign language tests in which the pupil may be asked to respond

in a foreign language to a number of spoken questions or be invited to describe in a foreign language the information contained in a photograph or some other stimulus material, or he may be asked to respond orally to a list of written questions in a foreign language. These are the conventional approaches to testing a pupil's oral ability in a foreign language and the pupil is likely to be assessed on such criteria as his comprehension of the questions and instructions, his vocabulary, his grammatical accuracy, his accent and style.

Second, there are oral examinations based on the non-language parts of the course. As was stated earlier, some schools use oral examinations as part of the assessment of a pupil's project, others use them as an alternative to conventional written examinations. The objectives are clearly different in both of these cases.

In an interesting concluding chapter of their book, *The New Social Studies*, Lawton and Dufour (1974) suggest that there are three parts to the procedure of assessing orally pupil's social thinking: (a) Content. What should the interview be about? What topics and subject-matter should be covered in it? (b) Technique. What sorts of questioning should occur? And what sorts of questions should be avoided? (c) Analysis. How can the record of the interview be used to make judgements about children's development of social concepts.

Although not written with formal external examinations in mind, this division has, nevertheless, some relevance for European Studies examinations. When an oral examination is tied to a CSE project then the substance of the questions to be asked of the candidate is already partially determined. In preparing the actual questions to be asked in the oral examination the examiner must distinguish between those closed questions which will yield an answer which can be judged to be correct or incorrect, and those open, subjective questions the answer to which are likely to be unpredictable. If the emphasis is on the former then the case for having an oral examination rather than a written examination is not particularly convincing. If the emphasis is on the latter types of questions then there will inevitably be many problems in awarding marks fairly and consistently.

When account is taken of the time required for oral examinations, the need to keep a balance between standard questions asked of all candidates and individual questions asked of particular candidates, plus the problem of marking fairly inarticulate and articulate candidates, it is not surprising that those teachers who employ oral examinations do not allocate many marks to them. However, it is possible to make a strong case for incorporating an oral into examination arrangements which examiners *may* use at their discretion without necessarily allocating any specified number of marks to it. The oral may then dispel any fears that an examiner has that a particular project is not *all* the pupil's own work, and it also serves as a useful check on a pupil's understanding of his project. If, however, it is necessary to check a pupil's project under examination conditions then including a compulsory question in the formal written examination would seem to be a much more efficient way of achieving this objective.

As Marshall and Hales (1971) comment 'When an oral response test is administered to an entire class, it is unlikely that any two students will be asked the same question under identical conditions. Most students will be asked only two or three questions, and their responses will be judged subjectively. Since students will be asked different questions, there will be no common criteria for comparing student responses. Furthermore, the sampling of content will be too limited to yield reliable or valid results. Consequently, the oral-response test so administered is likely to lack three important characteristics: validity, reliability and comparability of scores'.

Continuous Assessment

For many teachers continuous assessment is synonymous with course work. Course work includes homework assignments, a pupil's folder or notebook of lesson notes, fieldwork notes, class tests and end-of-term examinations. All of these may produce a list of marks which are totalled together to produce a final mark which is considered as a part of the total mark distribution for a CSE examination.

Hoste and Bloomfield (1975) distinguish two broad categories of techniques of continuous assessment: (a) Learning experience assessments, i.e. learning experiences which also form the basis of the assessment. An example of this within a European Studies course would be the interpretation of land use as shown on a foreign large-scale map equivalent to a British Ordnance Survey map: the pupil is assessed *as he learns* map interpretation. (b) Special assessment, i.e. special exercises conducted to sample learning. In this category are included homework assignments and classroom exercises designed to ensure that a pupil has acquired some particular information, skills or values.

This distinction is fundamental. Experience suggests that teachers of European Studies generally think of continuous assessment in terms of the second category. The explanation for this lies in the assumption that the content of European Studies courses, at least in the non-foreign language sector, is unstructured in any sequential way. It would appear that what is learned at the end of a course of European Studies is no more difficult than what is learned at the beginning—pupils simply accumulate more and more factual information. If this is so continuous assessment serves to reduce the sheer amount of information a pupil must remember for a terminal examination. But equally it could be argued that this only underestimates the place of skill-acquisition in European Studies courses.

For a teacher intending to examine pupils by continuous assessment the construction of an assessment schedule is essential. This should indicate the dates during a two-year course when assessment will take place and precisely what form of assessment will be employed. In CSE courses in which a substantial part of the total examination is via continuous assessment a schedule of this sort may be required by a moderator. A moderator may need to see the titles of assignments and the test papers before they are given to the candidates and, when continuous assessment includes learning experience assessments, it is likely that the moderator may wish to visit a school on several occasions during the life of a two-year course. It is obvious that the moderator's task of defining CSE grades for European Studies is particularly difficult when continuous assessment is a feature of a course. The most serious problem for both teacher and moderator is maintaining consistent marking over the period of the course. Without this it is virtually impossible to produce valid, reliable and comparable results at the end of the course, on which to base CSE grades.

European Studies and the Reform of Examinations
A successful pupil in GCE Ordinary level examinations can stay in school for a further two years and take GCE Advanced level examinations. This route is also appropriate for the successful CSE candidate who has passed several subjects at Grade 1 level. The pupil with CSE grades below this who decides to remain in school enters the sixth form and until very recently he would follow Advanced level courses in one or more subjects or he would take Ordinary level courses or re-sit his CSE examinations in order to try and improve his grades.

The need for a new examination structure for the successful CSE candidate has been acknowledged by examination boards and by the Schools Council. Simultaneously there has been a serious investigation of the possible reform of conventional sixth-form courses leading to new forms of examination. These investigations have been conducted by working parties of the Schools Council and the Standing Committee on University Entrance, supported by research studies carried out by the National Foundation for Educational Research and feasibility studies of new examinations by examination boards.

From this reformist activity a number of suggestions have emerged and these have generated much discussion and controversy. Among the suggested reforms are a common system of examinations at 16 plus, i.e.

the unification of CSE and GCE Ordinary level into a single examination (Schools Council 1971); a replacement of existing examinations by new examinations referred to as N and F (Schools Council 1973); the introduction of a post-CSE examination to be taken one year later and called the Certificate of Extended Education (Schools Council 1975a).

In Appendix A there is an example of a European Studies syllabus for a course to be examined under arrangements for the Certificate of Extended Education (CEE). The first candidates were examined for this course in 1975. CEE courses in various subjects have been organized in secondary schools on an experimental basis since 1972. The candidates have followed one year courses and these courses have been moderated in the same way as CSE Mode 1, 2 or 3 courses.

The Schools Council (1975) has outlined the form which CEE should take: 'The Schools Council decided that the proposed CEE would be designed primarily for students who have obtained CSE with grades 2-4. . . . The examinations would be available to schools, further education institutions and private individuals. . . . It was further decided that CEE should be designed for a one-year course, to suit the majority of those for whom it is intended. . . . Each course should aim to put a premium on understanding and application, together with the development of critical skills, in accordance with the needs of the more mature students. . . . Each syllabus would be designed to take up one-fifth of the time available for the main subjects of the curriculum. . . . It is anticipated that a five-point grading scale will be proposed by the Schools Council . . . with the lower boundary of the central grade being broadly equivalent to the CSE grade 1/2 boundary'.

The CEE offers considerable potential for the development of new European Studies courses. The pupils most likely to benefit are:

1 those who have already taken CSE or GCE Ordinary level European Studies courses since they can take their studies a stage further, so enabling them to broaden their field of study or deepen their study of selected topics;

2 those who have taken geography, history and a modern language at CSE or GCE Ordinary level because for them European Studies offers an inter-disciplinary study in which they may synthesize the knowledge and skills already gained in their uni-disciplinary courses;

3 those who are studying European Studies in addition to other area studies, e.g. American Studies or Caribbean Studies, for CEE;

4 those who are studying a group of social studies or social science subjects, e.g. politics, sociology, history and/or geography, for CEE;

5   those following courses for CEE with a strong bias towards the physical sciences who would take a European Studies course as a minority time course;

6   those following courses for CEE with an emphasis on foreign languages who would benefit from an area study focusing on Europe.

Conclusion

For the enthusiastic advocate of European Studies as a serious curriculum innovation there are many convincing reasons why more and more courses should be established in secondary schools. Although the arguments have been forcibly expressed in conferences and in-service courses the spread of European Studies courses has been slow and confined very largely to pupils in the lower ability ranges within the final years of compulsory schooling.

Although there are teachers who would argue that European Studies courses ought not to be externally examined, and this case is frequently argued in discussing courses for sixth formers, it is the pressure to provide the school leaver with paper qualifications that has ensured the proliferation of CSE European Studies courses. When considering the curriculum of the school leaver the number of these courses moderated in an examinations board is dwarfed by the number of courses in such areas as design and craft, home economics and social studies. Analysis of the results obtained in CSE European Studies examinations reveals a high proportion of candidates attaining the lowest categories of grades—Grade 5 and ungraded. This has created an image of European Studies as being a curriculum area suitable for pupils of the lowest ability. Such an image must inevitably make the courses less attractive to pupils of high ability and to their teachers.

The provision of curriculum materials designed for the low ability pupil may ease the teaching problem for those teachers of European Studies who find themselves confronted by children who have been judged, or who have judged themselves, as unlikely to succeed in French or German, geography or history in GCE or CSE Mode 1 courses. But the materials themselves may serve to perpetuate the image. The same may be true of the amount of energy and time devoted by teachers to designing and refining CSE courses. Designing a Mode 3 CSE course can be seen as an ad hoc measure to solve a single school's particular teaching problems. Rarely is the creation of such a European Studies course seen as part of an overall curriculum plan, as one of a series of related courses which contribute to the child's total school education.

Viewed positively, as I indicated in the opening chapter, European Studies has a valuable part to play in the common curriculum of the secondary school pupil. The whole concept of the common curriculum in which individual subjects or courses fulfil distinctive aims for children of a particular age group can be seen to disintegrate in the fourth and fifth years of secondary schooling where children are filtered into academic and non-academic subjects, where they are streamed and setted according to abilities defined by the requirements of external examinations and where groups of children may be defined as non-examinees or marginal examinees. If European Studies courses are to be taken seriously then the case for making them central to the curriculum of the secondary school must be argued seriously.

The case rests upon two broad foundations. First, European Studies, by focusing upon political, social, cultural and economic aspects of life in Europe, extends the child's knowledge and understanding beyond a local and national base and provides the opportunity to study European issues from various academic perspectives. A European Studies course ought to place the child's local experience into a broader international framework. With Britain's increasing involvement in European affairs the aims of education for citizenship and education for international understanding become closely linked in a European context.

Secondly, since a full understanding of European affairs requires familiarity with at least one mainland European language plus the knowledge and insights gained from travel and observing the details of foreign environments and meeting the nationals of foreign countries, European Studies provides a bridge between the areas of study in schools broadly described as the humanities and the study of modern languages. This bridge, if it can be successfully constructed, brings together the traditions and expertise of two long established curriculum areas. These may gain more than they lose from a thoroughgoing synthesis. Whatever gains may be attained are likely to be most noticeable for the pupils who reach the highest levels of intellectual achievement on both sides of the bridge. It is recognition of this assumption which probably explains the attraction of European Studies for teachers and students in higher education.

Some would argue that provision is already made for the first of these two foundations in existing history and geography courses. And the counter-argument stresses that many pupils are obliged to choose between studying either geography or history, and in both of these courses more attention is paid to aspects of British life than to Europe.

Other arguments are promulgated by those who see Europe as being too small a conception in a contracting world. If the world is conceived as a global village then nothing short of world studies should be contemplated. Thus European Studies would be acceptable within a larger course in which American Studies, Caribbean Studies or Asian Studies play a part. European Studies would be taught consecutively or concurrently with these other area studies. Counter-arguments to these arrangements must be based on the uniqueness of European life though, as yet, there is little evidence in the schools that this is a major substantive area of exploration. Europe has been selected as the continent for study principally for narrow, political reasons, or for the simple reason that teachers of French, German or Spanish are employed in schools.

In the preface it was stated that if European Studies courses can be mounted successfully then they may be seen eventually as a great stride towards effective world studies courses. Until European Studies ceases to be considered as a course suitable only for the school leavers who are the most difficult to teach it will not be taken seriously by pupils, teachers, parents and employers. It appears likely that the language element in European Studies courses will either be made optional or will disappear altogether and that this trend, which is already evident, will accelerate as the cost of foreign travel increases. In this way one of the two foundations may cease to exist. The humanities components of courses may well be enveloped either in social studies, environmental studies, political studies and world studies, or in the more conventional, though rapidly changing, subjects: geography, history and economics.

At present there is increasing information about course content and a continuing flow of curriculum materials to support courses. There is no evidence of what actually takes place in European Studies classrooms and, in particular, we know little of what is learned and how it is learned in European Studies. Examinable projects and examination papers clearly do not constitute the whole of a pupil's learning. There is considerable scope for serious enquiry into the activity called teaching European Studies, and the results of such enquiry should provide some clues to the solution of the important problem of just what constitutes *successful* European Studies teaching.

APPENDIX A

Examples of European
Studies Courses

1 European Studies: A Source for an Integrated Studies Syllabus
This course outline was published as a booklet by Oxfordshire Education Committee in 1970 and it was circulated widely amongst teachers throughout Britain. Oxfordshire has long been active in promoting a wide array of exchanges and links with other parts of Europe and this course outline must be viewed as one part of the complicated Study and Travel Scheme initiated by the local education authority. It should be noted that since this outline was published in 1970 several European Studies courses have been mounted in Oxfordshire secondary schools and many of the courses have developed beyond the suggestions made in this introductory outline.

OXFORDSHIRE EDUCATION COMMITTEE

EUROPEAN STUDIES

A Source for an Integrated Studies Syllabus

This pool of ideas from which a CSE Mode 3 syllabus in European Studies can be selected was prepared by an ad hoc working party during a week-end at Yenworthy in January 1970. It is offered to those schools that would like to draw from this collection of ideas for their own integrated syllabus in European Studies.

Members of the Working Party believe that it is necessary that students following a course in European Studies should be able to communicate with their continental friends: that they should have some ability in a continental language and a knowledge of a basic minimum of fact relevant to life in modern Europe. And in addition that students should be able to pursue studies of particular interest to some depth.

It was hoped that this course would be taught by a team in which language teachers would work closely with specialists in Home Economics, History and

120

Geography, together with the assistance of Art and Music teachers, etc., when appropriate. It is strongly recommended that the course should include a piece of assessable practical work, which could represent either a complete topic or part of a topic.

The course envisaged consists of a compulsory core occupying about 40% of the study time available and tested by examination. The core contains the basic minimum of facts required. The remaining 60% of the time would be taken up by a study of one or more of the optional topics. Selection, study and assessment of the topic work should be as flexible as possible. Topics could be studied by individuals or as group projects with either continuous or final assessment. But wherever possible topic work should be centred on the life of one family, it should be directed at the present, to a small area, and to the readily verifiable. It is envisaged that few schools would wish to choose from more than four separate topics, some might choose from only one or two.

Schools wishing to use this type of syllabus should add to the core study a carefully selected series of studies from the optional topics. These should be selected on the basis of

(i) the material available,
(ii) staff and pupil interest,
(iii) the need to pursue a balanced study of Europe to some depth.

The Working Party considers that an intensive study of a few aspects is preferable to an attempt to cover too wide a field.

GENERAL INTRODUCTION

This CSE course in European Studies is intended to provide students with the basic minimum of knowledge required to meet and talk to their continental friends and to enable them to study one or more aspects of their way of life.

The core, which is intended to be compulsory, occupies 40% of the study time available, should be tested by examination, and includes some knowledge of a foreign language. The remaining 60% is taken up by the study of one or more of the optional topics. It is essential that the choice of topics, their study, and the way they are presented, should give the opportunity for a balanced study to some depth of various aspects of European life and culture. No GCE or CSE candidate in a foreign language should take the optional language topic in that language.

It is suggested that the course would most profitably be prepared and taught by a team of teachers working closely together preferably in a timetable 'block'.

The presentation of an aspect of a topic as a project should be encouraged, as should a group project, so long as it is assured that each member of the group has made a full contribution.

1 'CORE' STUDY

Pupils who follow a course in European Studies over at least a two year period should have assimilated a body of knowledge about Europe in general. This should be an essential part of the course and to this end a compulsory examination should be set to test this 'core' material. It is recommended that candidates who fail to reach a pass standard on this compulsory paper should not be graded higher than Grade 4.

The examination tests:
- (a) their ability to comprehend a basic minimum of words and phrases in a European language;
- (b) their knowledge of the basic geography of Europe;
- (c) their knowledge of the political developments in Europe since 1945 and of the present situation;
- (d) their understanding of the major religious groupings and which languages are spoken in which countries.

These aspects are explained in more detail below. It is suggested that 40% of the total marks be allotted for this section and that candidates should obtain 2/5ths of the marks on this paper if they are to reach a pass standard. The material lends itself to objective testing and out of a 100 question test some 5 marks could be allocated to topic D, the remainder being equally divided between sections A, B and C.

SECTION A. LANGUAGE

(i) *Material to be learned in an active context*
- (a) About 30 common verbs in the present tense, question and answer form in the various persons and in the negative (emphasis on understanding and pronunciation).
- (b) The basic question words (e.g. quand, ou, comment, qui, quel, etc.).
- (c) Numbers, days, dates, times.
- (d) About 20 simple adjectives.
- (e) Common nouns dealing with family, furniture, clothes, body, travel, food and drink, entertainment.
- (f) The most common idioms not included above.

(ii) *Suggested methods of testing (using French as an example)*
- (a) French questions involving one word or very basic answers in French.
- (b) Passage of reading as pronunciation exercise.
- (c) Questions in English to be answered in English on:
  - (a) a French passage read out loud by the teacher;
  - (b) a French passage read by the pupil.
- (d) Some questions to be answered in English may be on the 'core' history and geography material.

SECTION B. THE GEOGRAPHY OF EUROPE
(a) *The position of Europe*
Relationship to other continents.
(b) *The major physical features*
The main mountain chains as barriers and the plains and river valleys as routeways.

(c) *The map of Europe*
Mapping of the major countries and the significant towns.
(d) *European communications*
Routes from Britain into Europe. (The distance being worked out in terms of time by road and rail and not miles.) The major routeways across Europe ('E' roads) means of crossing major barriers, i.e. the Channel, the Alps.
(e) *The importance of climatic differences*
The significant differences between the Arctic north and the Mediterranean south, the maritime west and the continental east.
(f) *Contemporary European projects*
i.e. the Channel tunnel, Concorde, the European airbus, etc.

SECTION C. RECENT POLITICAL DEVELOPMENTS
(a) Friends or enemies in the 2nd World War.
    (a)   Who fought on whose side and why?
    (b)   Which countries remained neutral and why?
    (c)   The growth of resistance/the formation of the Allied Powers.
(b) Friends and enemies after the war.
    (a)   Why Russia and her allies quarrelled.
    (b)   How Europe looked in 1945:
        Berlin divided by occupation;
        Europe divided by the Marshall Plan.
(c) The growth of European organizations.
    In the west: BENELUX; EEC/EFTA; Council of Europe; NATO.
    In the east: COMECON; The Warsaw Pact.

SECTION D. RELIGION AND LANGUAGE
(a) The major European churches and the countries in which they are predominant—their effects on social attitudes.
(b) The major European languages and the areas in which they are spoken—countries which are bilingual/multilingual and the consequences.

OPTIONAL TOPICS

Introduction

60% of the total marks are allocated for work in one or more of the optional topics. The choice of subject, the number of topics studied and their method of presentation should be determined by the need to pursue a balanced study of the European way of life to some depth.

Topics should be tackled from a personal angle and, as far as possible, in a practical and imaginative manner. The important general theme is the business of living in Europe here and now.

Topic 1, The Family: How People Live, is so important that it should be considered an essential study where a visit abroad is envisaged and evidence of this study should be available if required.

TOPIC 1. THE FAMILY: How People Live
In this topic historical, geographical or sociological information should be given where it is helpful, but this must be subsidiary to the central theme of living in Europe here and now. Practical work in the Home Economics Department should include such things as cooking, table-laying, behaviour at meals, introduction, etc., and there is a great scope both here and in the classroom for role play.

This topic needs to be taken as a team project in which the teacher of Home Economics works closely with the teacher of French/German and any other member of staff (e.g. an assistant, if there is one, who has a good first-hand knowledge of the area chosen for particular study). If the school is lucky enough to have a continental type restaurant in the vicinity a useful contact could be made with the personnel.

Examining and assessing this section
A written test of the traditional type would seem to be irrelevant. Assessing this section could usefully be based on the following:
  (1)   Role play, improvisation, dialogue based on practical situations about which the child has learnt and which he might encounter, e.g. breakfast in a French home; scene in a café; a formal visit; dating; being faced with a menu, etc., etc.
  (2)   Continuous assessment of course work, particularly useful where practical activities such as cookery are involved.
  (3)   The presentation of *either* a course folder based on one aspect which has particularly interested the student, e.g. French cooking—*or*, where there has been a foreign visit, a folder or display of work based on personal experience abroad. (There is no reason why this should not be a group effort.)

It may be useful to compare a family typical of the area in which the school is situated with one typical of the area to be visited and of special interest in Europe. The following headings may provide helpful guide-lines in the exploring of these differences and similarities, but it cannot be too strongly stressed that approaches must be relevant and practical:

  (a)   *What is expected of the young adult and what he/she should expect*
        How a student visiting a French/German home should behave. Customs and courtesies, including greetings, handshaking, conversation at meals, outings with hosts and family. When to write/send flowers. How to address elders, contemporaries, members of the opposite sex.
        Dating. How to make oneself agreeable without giving one's escort the wrong idea. A word about wine. How to fend off unsuitable advances.
        Finding one's way round the town. Shopping. Ordering coffee or a meal in a café. At the post office. Travelling and public transport. Using the syndicat d'initiative or other information centre.

  (b)   *Homes and families*
        Kinds of dwelling; amenities, fittings, furnishings—especially

bathrooms (bidet), bedding (duvet) and other things which students might find strange.

(c) *Eating and drinking*
Water, coffee and wine: what to expect. A typical breakfast, etc. Influence of working patterns on meals—traditional food/convenience foods—as in England. Pride in regional dishes. Economical house-keeping—soups, etc. What is food cooked in, on and by? Any special foods, customs, songs for feast days—e.g. Christmas, Easter, birthdays.

Practical work to include continental cookery (whole meal projects) with guidance on how to lay the table, which implements to use and the way in which they will be used, the order in which food is eaten, with emphasis on differences where relevant (e.g. lack of side plate; place of cheese and ice cream, etc.).

TOPIC 2. DEVELOPMENT: Family Life In:

(a) Under-developed areas of Southern Europe. Examples—Fund for the South (Mezzogiorno in Italy). Reasons for under-development, steps being taken to improve the situation, not only in terms of land and employment on it, but also in terms of providing the industrial, commercial, communications and social situation. Examples in the Midi in France. Development in the Rhone Valley and in the Languedoc—the 'Californie Française'.

(b) Boom Towns, e.g. Linköping or Wolfsburg. High salaries and how people live the 'good life'. Advantages and disadvantages of working for a super company. Advantages and disadvantages of a town depending on a single industry.

(c) Developing Coastal Lands. Example—the Rhine Delta (dams, reclamation of land, new resources and amenities). Reference made to the Wash in England.

(d) EEC development areas. Reference to development areas in Britain.

TOPIC 3. POPULATION: The Changing Pattern

(a) Migration of people from areas with poor prospects to where there is work—where from and why, and where to and why. Desirable and undesirable consequences. 'We are from the South'. Examples—Southern Italians to Northern Italy, Sweden, Belgium and Switzerland. Greeks and Turks to Germany. Movement of trained technologists into developing areas.

Refugees of Europe—from behind the Iron Curtain. Example—East Germans and Berliners to West Germany. Actual example—Neugablonz—costume jewellery and glass. Approach—problems of resettlement of a refugee family.

(b) People to cities:
  (i) Why people leave the country to live and work in the cities. Rural depopulation. Problems of urbanization.

    (ii)   The Big Cities—where and why, including the newer international cities such as Brussels and Geneva, the conurbations such as Randstad.
Dealing with overspill populations—example, the 1965 Paris plan as compared with British New Towns. Method—suggested entry into the topic via 'Family X move from A to B' as
    (1)   migrants,
    (2)   refugees,
    (3)   a rural family.
What would they stand to gain? What would be their problems? (Comparisons to be made constantly with Britain.)

TOPIC 4. ENERGY: The Changing Pattern of Energy Use and its Influence on Social Development

(a)   Heating one's home. Comparison of heating methods in different countries (include degree of heating). Reference to situation in UK.

(b)   The coalfields—distribution. Example—the Ruhr: changes occurring. (Reasons for the decline in coal consumption and effects on coalfields. Refer to situation in Britain.)

(c)   The discovery of oil and natural gas.
    (i)   resulting changes;
    (ii)   transporting oil and gas. Examples: Gas in Holland; Oil and gas in Germany; The Saharan oil and gas and how it is being transported to markets in Europe; The North Sea strike and its effects—methane gas transport to British Isles.

(d)   Development of water resources for electricity. Example—one example from the USSR—the river Angara and the Rance scheme in Brittany.

(e)   Nuclear Power. What conditions are required in setting up a nuclear power station; the nuclear power stations in Britain; the Swedish developments; the Euratom policy of the EEC.

TOPIC 5. AGRICULTURE: How it is Affected by Political and Economic Systems in which the Farmer Manages his Land. The Relationship Between Agricultural and Social Development

(a)   A Danish Co-operative Farm—how the co-op principle and close government supervision ensures the continuing prosperity of the Danish farmer. A typical day and year. The Folk Schools.

(b)   Collective Farm in the USSR. State farm in the USSR. How each type is run and how this affects the lives of the people living on them. Typical day and year.

(c)   A Peasant Farm in the West, e.g. Centre of Brittany. Typical day and year. How farm consolidation programmes affect the typical family. How agricultural prices negotiated with other Common Market countries affect the farmer.

(d)   Agricultural Development. The Agrarian Revolution and its continuance today has effects on farming methods in various regions

of Europe. Food producers often face similar problems through climate, landforms and customs of inheritance.
(e) The agricultural policy of the UK and the effects of our going into the Common Market on (a) the farm, (b) the consumer. Suggested approach—a visit to a supermarket or going on a spending spree in Britain and an EEC country.

TOPIC 6. INDUSTRY: Work and the Influence on Family Life
(a) Working in a typical factory. A typical day in 'heavy' and 'light' industry, using examples from Bavaria and the Jura. Comparison with home area.
(b) The changing heavy industry of Western Europe. Examples—
   (i) The heavy industrial regions of the EEC and how they are being affected by the policies of the Coal and Steel Community (include movement of coal and iron ore, the Moselle Canal).
   (ii) The shift of heavy industry to the coast. Examples—Europort, Dunkirk, Marseille.
   (iii) The motor industry in Western Europe—location, including examples from Britain—comparison of French, Italian, German, Swedish and British cars.
   (iv) Industry in Franche Comté and Switzerland: how to make the most out of little. Industries based on technical knowledge.

TOPIC 7. TRANSPORT: Changes Occurring in Transport and Their Influences on Social Conditions
Suggested approach:
  A How one gets from this country to various places in Europe and how to prepare oneself for the journey.
  B Advantages and disadvantages of various ways of getting there.
   (1) Railways: Effects of electrification; Effects of poltical boundaries on.
   (2) Tunnels: New developments in Alpine countries, the proposed 'Chunnel'.
   (3) Motorways: German autobahn, Italian autostradas, the Europa routes. Advantages and disadvantages of motorways.
   (4) Navigable Waterways: Changes occurring on Rhine—Rhone.
   (5) Ports:
     (a) Ferry services (various) from Britain to Europe.
     (b) Container services.
     (c) New superports: Europort, Antwerp, Marseille.
   (6) Air Transport: Eurobus jet.

TOPIC 8. TOURISM
(a) Why go abroad?
(b) Where to go: playgrounds of Europe—Mediterranean—Adriatic coastline—Switzerland/Austria—Nordic countries—behind the Iron Curtain.

(c) How to go and when to go: Package Tours—Camping—Off-season—Various ways of getting there.

(d) The British abroad—how they see themselves—comparing the image of each country—expressing holiday wants to tourist agency—how we see them—experiences abroad.
An examination of typical holidays in the style of BBC TV 'Holidays 70'.

(e) Planning and going on a holiday.

TOPIC 9. THE FAMILY

(Examples and comparisons can be made right across Europe, chosen according to similarity or contrast of situation and background. Probably pupils making an exchange visit would base their work on this.)

(1) *Wandering families*
Reference to first settlements and reasons for their choice (safety, availability of food, etc.).
Why do people move on? What do they live in? What happens to their earnings, status and children's education? What language? What customs?

(a) *Nomads by choice.* Tramps and their codes, gypsies.

(b) *Nomadic occupations.* Going where the work is, scrap metal, vegetable and fruit picking/gypsies making clothes pegs, fairground men, circus families, drovers, bargees, musicians, actors, civil servants, academics (the brain-drain).

(c) *Movement as a result of social and economic change.* Growth of canals and railways; industrial revolution causing displacement and enabling mobility. (Vagrants even in Tudor times; 'The Wandering Scholars' in medieval Europe and mobility amongst the clergy). Closing of coal mines, mechanization of farms, computer 'take-over', re-training schemes (Italians working for Volkswagen and Irish on the motorways). Drift from the land, immigration/emigration.

(d) *Effects of war and persecution.* Evacuees (country to country, town to country). Refugees (Jews, Poles . . . Czechs). The skills and crafts they have taken with them (Huguenot clockmakers, weavers). The foods they have brought, and our changed habits. History of Jews.

(e) *Problems from movements.* Language, but also social customs and the dilemma of the bearded Sikh ambulance man, betrousered Muslim schoolgirls; multi-racial schools and the methods they are employing (see Schools Council WP13 and its bibliography).

(2) *Settled homes*
Compare similar families, e.g. both professional or both working class in England and, say, France/Austria/Norway, etc. Comparison of garden, car, help in the house. Climatic influence such as a siesta, midday meal, etc. Do both parents work?

(3) *Type of dwelling*
Planning affected by location, climate, raw materials, cost, need, whether grandparents share the home, etc. Owned or rented? Do countries vary over amount of privacy required and respected? Tied property, council houses?

(4) *Family relationships*
Role of the mother and of the father as affected by religion and tradition. Attitude to the old and to children. Who inherits land or money? Who brings up the children? Who looks after the baby? Does the family go out as a unit or separately for leisure? Are parents on the whole respected? Does the family go out for meals?

(5) *The family and the community*
The individual's rights and responsibilities. Voting, taxation, national service, jury service.
The Community's protection for babies and children (health, schooling), for workers (wage protection, unemployment benefits), for consumers (housing, price subsidies, transport), for the old (pensioners).
The historical growth of welfare provisions, differences between city and country areas, the effect of political and religious traditions.
Voluntary organizations, e.g. Samaritans, NSPCC and their counterparts.

(6) *Class structures*
Aristocracies of birth/money/brain? e.g. Russia. Examples of continuing feudalism, peasantry. Effect of national educational system.
Degree to which birth determines opportunity. Problem of children alienated from parents by education.

TOPIC 10. RELIGION

The pupil's own religion—friends and family—personal knowledge.
The priest and local religious leaders—role in community, separateness.
The role of the priest elsewhere—women priests, worker priests, married priests, priests in Italy, Ireland, etc. (Don Camillo).

The likely religion of a family in selected European countries:
e.g. Spain, Greece, Sweden (also Bavaria and 'link' areas).
Consider areas, occupations, temperament.
The main religions of Europe and different religious practices:
e.g. Roman Catholic churches, Protestant churches, Orthodox churches, Jews, other religions.
Alternatives—atheism, materialism, witchcraft.
Consider festivals, churchgoing, services, the look of church buildings, differences in music, religious art.
Some study of:
the growth of Christendom, the Reformation and its spread—Luther, Calvin; the Churches and problems caused in the 19th century by new ideas

and movements—Marx, Darwin, democracy, industrial growth; relations between the main European Churches today.

How does religion affect behaviour?
Sunday observance—shops, pubs. On the continent, football as a 20th century 'religion'. Grace at meals.

Religion affecting dress—what to wear in different churches and countries, no bikinis in Spain. More formal dances in Europe—how it can affect manners between boys and girls, and between parents and children. Marriage, birth control. Religion and morals. Degree of censorship in countries due to religion. Religion and the ending of licensed prostitution in late 19th century England. Why licensed prostitution allowed in some European countries today? The Scandinavian outlook. Comparative suicide rates and strength of religion. Religion and persecution. How far would a child go to maintain his own beliefs? How far would he tolerate differences? The persecution of Churches—in the past; today (the Inquisition; the Churches and Nazi Germany; Churches and Communist European states today). Conscientious Objectors in 1939/45 war, or in Spain today. Interviews with known ones—tribunals in GB up to the end of National Service. The Churches and political parties in European countries. Closer links than in England. Why?

TOPIC 11. EMPLOYMENT

(Great care must be taken in the choice of studies from Topics 11-14. They should be attempted only when first hand information is readily available to the teacher and when there is the opportunity to express the work in an imaginative way.)

Proceeding from the patterns of employment in Britain to a consideration of the situation in certain countries or areas of the continent. Conditions in the area likely to be visited by the children should be studied and, in addition, examples from one agricultural, one industrial, one commercial district and one in a communist country. Case studies of employees will reveal differences and similarities most effectively.

(a) *Method of Employment*
    A class of children could be asked to find patterns of employment of own parents: self-employed, small firm, large firm, state. Comparisons could then be made with patterns in other countries.

(b) *Major occupations*
    Compiling basic statistics and graphs showing employment in different countries in: agriculture, mining, manufacture, professions, civil service and other major occupations. Comparisons could be made between particular industries.

(c) *Working conditions*
    Comparison of hours and conditions, wages and wages value. Case studies could be used to show the difference of the lives of farmers, miners, factory employees, clerks, etc., in different countries.

(d) *Trade Unions*
    Comparisons of the way Unions affect workers (subscriptions and securities) and their legal position within the state.

TOPIC 12. EDUCATION (NB—See the introduction to Topic 11)

A comparison of the typical daily routine, school work and prospects of school children of several selected countries, with special reference to the exchange areas. The comparisons would attempt to show the influence of history, geography, religion and political ideology as well as considering the consequences of the differing educational patterns.

Suitable countries might be: Britain; Poland (communist); Spain (strong Catholic element); Sweden (extensive state influence); plus the area likely to be visited by the school children.

(a) *The course of a typical child's education*
Infant; Primary; Secondary; Further education
showing
   (a) ages at which changes are made;
   (b) whether there is selection and special schooling;
   (c) examination system;
   (d) private and religious schooling—numbers involved;
   (e) co-educational or not.

(b) *The course of a typical child's day and curriculum*
Comparison of timetables and available choices noticing especially: sports, languages learnt, religion, practical subjects.

(c) *State influence—*
leading from control of curriculum and permitted flexibility to system of payment for schools, employment of teachers.

(d) *Additional studies might be made of—*
Universities and students: student protest;
Progressive and experimental schools;
Vocational training provisions.

TOPIC 13. EUROPE AND THE WORLD
(NB—See the introduction to Topic 11)

(a) *An expansion of the 'core' syllabus*
i.e. Europe as a 'Third Force'—could Europe become as strong as Russia or the USA if united? What advantages would there be? What attempts to unite Europe have there been? (Council of Europe, etc.). What economic links have been made, and how do these affect international relations? (e.g. iron and steel federation, EEC, EFTA, COMECON, etc.). Also international groupings that go outside Europe, such as NATO.

(b) *Links with past colonies*
Possibly choose three European countries and trace the history of their connections with a colony, e.g. Britain and Canada, or Botswana; France and Algeria, or Senegal; Denmark and Greenland.
(Draw maps of explorations, imports and exports between the two countries, social and educational exchanges. Conclusions on motive of parent country. Advantages and disadvantages of independence, if any.)

(c) *History of slavery*
Which European countries imported slaves, and from where? Which ports; enquire into prices, conditions of life, enslavement of Huguenots. When and where did anti-slavery protests begin? Attitude of Churches, attitude of missionaries.

(d) *Overseas Aid*
How rich is Europe compared to rest of world? What percentage of GNP goes on helping underdeveloped countries? How do, say, Britain and Italy compare over this?

(e) *Division of Europe into colonial powers and others*
Reasons for this.

(f) *Coloured immigration*
Differences over regulations and countries of origin, e.g. West Indies—Britain, Dutch E. Indies—Holland, Algerians—France. Attitudes and problems.

TOPIC 14. GOVERNMENT (NB—See the introduction to Topic 11)
Political systems, democracy, communism, dictatorships—choice of Hitler, Mussolini, Franco? What prevents our Prime Minister becoming one? Role played by President and/or Prime Minister.
Types of regime.
Europe since the 1939-45 war.
What are the problems involved in Britain's present application to join the EEC?
Detailed study of one European political system including local government.
Projects on local government or local government schemes.
Portrait of or interviews with mayor—how did the local swimming pool get built?
The role of the individual.
Political personalities can be subjects of interest.

TOPIC 15. EUROPEAN CULTURAL LIFE
This option contains a recommended minimum of investigation together with a number of additional themes of which *two* should be chosen.
The teacher may cover these two themes in any manner he thinks fit but investigation by the pupil should play a large part in this work, and where appropriate active participation by the pupil should be encouraged. Evidence can be gathered either on a visit to a foreign country or from a pen friend, or from various sources in Britain. Rather than the compilation of lists or dossiers, the teacher should try to foster attempts to understand, probe, or investigate a part of the theme on a fairly narrow front.
We do not envisage questions being set on any part of this option but assessment should be on evidence of study particularly of work in art, music, etc.
In view of this it may prove possible for specialists in these and other subjects to help in the work in some of the themes in this option.

Throughout the work comparisons should be made between different countries.

(a) *Compulsory minimum* (to be covered in the two years)
  (i) The viewing of one European film, preferably continental.
  (ii) One visit to an art gallery to see different schools of European painting.
  (iii) Reading or seeing a performance of one European book or play in translation.
  (iv) Visiting one building of artistic merit.
  Personal comment or research on each of these of about three pages.

(b) *Suggested themes* (*two* to be covered)
  Active participation in the subject of these themes to be encouraged. Evidence of study to be produced, but a large scale project not required.
  (i) *Group or individual activity.* The performance in school of: European songs, instrumental music, dances, extracts from plays, etc.
  (ii) *Europe at leisure.* The cinema; pop music; hobbies.
  The attitude to leisure—(many European city dwellers living in flats).
  Annual and occasional holidays—activities, e.g. sports, winter sports, climbing, boating, camping, etc.
  Social customs—eating and drinking out, shopping, parks and amusements, Christmas and Easter, etc.
  (iii) *Looking and listening.* National flavours in painting and music; opera and ballet and their place in the life of the country; music making, dancing and folk song; costumes; fashion.
  (iv) *Evidence of design*
    (a) Domestic design—e.g. Scandinavian tableware.
    (b) Civil engineering—e.g. motorways, bridges, barrages, tunnels, etc.
    (c) Domestic architecture—e.g. houses and flats; town planning.
  (v) *What's happening in the Arts.* Pop art, kinetic art, musique concrète, jazz idioms, literature.
  (vi) *Sport.* National preferences; European football teams, training, style of play; athletics and personalities.
  (vii) *Press and radio.* Comparison of teenage magazines, analysis of style of presentation, continental radio programmes, types of advertising (compare also with Britain).

TOPIC 16. HISTORY

An investigation of the influences of the past which have helped to shape modern Europe. Emphasis on European movements and the unity of European culture rather than separate national developments.

Study of this topic would consist of two sections: (a) the broad outline, forming a framework in which (b) studies in depth of limited aspects, could be fitted.

(a) *Outline*
What the major European movements were and when they occurred. The Roman Empire, Dark Ages, Charlemagne and the Holy Roman Empire, Medieval Europe (cultural units, feudal rivalry), the Renaissance, the Reformation, the Great Dynasties (Hapsburg, Bourbon), revolutions and the decline of monarchy, nationalism and 19th century rivalries, imperial expansion overseas, 20th century conflicts.
Work on the outline should be kept very simple. Testing could be by one word answer, chart, and map testing.

(b) A study in depth of one or more of the movements listed above, stressing why these movements occurred and their effects on modern Europe. This work would most suitably be presented as an individual or group project.

TOPIC 17. LANGUAGE
(1) *Material and structures*
Four tenses expected: Present, Perfect, Future, Imperfect. Imperative, Negative, Interrogative.
Agreement of adjectives; object, interrogative and relative pronouns.
Vocabulary and structure to approximately half the standard of CSE in the given language.

(2) *Method of testing* (suggested)
  (a) A linguistic project such as a playlet, set of correspondence or poem(s) in a foreign language.
     or
     Creative writing (free composition) (½ hour).
  (b) Comprehension (½ hour).
     (i) Foreign language extract and questions and answers in that language.
  or (ii) A harder extract with questions and answers in English.
  or (iii) Passage to be translated into English.
  or (iv) Aural comprehension passage: questions and answers in English.
  or (v) Multiple choice questions on oral language extract.
  (c) Oral (15 minutes).
     (i) General questions.
     (ii) Questions on a given topic *or* on project.
     (iii) Passage in foreign language to be read.

2   The Somerset Integrated European Studies Syllabus
One year after the publication of the Oxfordshire course outline a working party of teachers and advisers set up by the Somerset Education Committee issued its findings. The working party was led by E. J. Neather, at that time adviser on modern languages for Somerset.

The following extract from the working party's integrated European Studies syllabus should be read as the first stage in the evolution of the working party's thinking about curriculum development in European Studies and its more recent published suggestions are taken up at the end of the extract.

THE AIMS OF THE SOMERSET WORKING PARTY

The final recommendations of the working party were arrived at after a good deal of discussion and exploration of possibilities. We were lucky to draw on the expertise and experience of a number of teachers from a wide range of subject disciplines. We attempted at all times to bear certain principles in mind. Whatever changes might be made to the suggestions put forward, when they are adapted to the circumstances of individual schools, we should hope that these principles would be adhered to.

First, we have been at pains to keep in view always the need to cross subject barriers and to evolve a truly integrated syllabus.

Secondly, we have been anxious to encourage the methods which seem to us appropriate for such studies, i.e. ample opportunity for individual work and personal research. We also hope that the course will be sufficiently flexible for teachers to take advantage of events and topics of immediate interest, as they hit the headlines.

The provision of a Mode 3 CSE syllabus was a subject of some controversy in the working party. The place at which European Studies should be brought into the school, the age and ability of children for whom the course was intended, these are subjects which formed an essential part of our early discussions. We opted for a CSE syllabus to give shape to our discussions and to concentrate our minds. We believe that the principles here set out can serve not only as a source for individual schools to produce a Mode 3 syllabus of their own, but also as a basis for further adaptations to different age groups and abilities. It is with such adaptations in mind, particularly the needs of younger secondary school pupils, non-examination pupils and sixth formers, that the working party is to maintain a standing committee to continue its work and develop its thinking. This standing committee will also be available to receive feed-back from schools, to amend these proposals in the light of such feed-back, and to provide an information service on available resources.

The Aims of the Syllabus

The integrated European Studies syllabus has three fundamental aims.
(1)   To achieve an understanding of contemporary European societies.
(2)   To prepare pupils for European visits and exchanges.
(3)   To increase pupil motivation by an emphasis on learner-participation in the Studies.

Syllabus Content

Section 1: A Compulsory Common Core
1A   The Study of One European Language.
1B   The Changing Map of Europe.
1C   Sample Studies of European Societies.

Section 2: Course Work Topics
2A   Aspects of National Ways of Life within European Countries.
2B   Inter-European Studies.

Examination Structure
The *Compulsory Common Core* will be examined by THREE written papers, 1A, 1B and 1C. Each paper will contribute up to 10% of the total awarded marks for the examination. The Compulsory Common Core will contribute up to 30% of the total awarded marks for the examination.
  Paper 1A   1½ hours (written and oral).
  Paper 1B   1½ hours.
  Paper 1C   1½ hours.
  The *course work topics* will be assessed and will contribute up to 70% of the total awarded marks for the examination. Not less than THREE and not more than FIVE topics may be submitted.
  Not more than ONE topic may be selected from any one country in Section 2A. At least TWO of the submitted topics must be selected from Section 2B.

Time Allocation for Studies
The European Studies Course is expected to extend over FIVE academic terms. Candidates should be allocated SEVEN 40-minute lessons (or the equivalent) per week. Each Section should receive the following time allowance:

Section 1: The Compulsory Common Core

Section 1A. *The Study of One European Language*
80 minutes per week, divided into at least two sessions, for FIVE terms.

Section 1B. *The Changing Map of Europe*
FIVE 40-minute lessons (or equivalent) per week over ONE-HALF term. As this is the introductory course it is advised that the first half-term of study be devoted to this section.

Section 1C. *Sample Studies of European Societies*
TWO 40-minute lessons (or equivalent) per week over FOUR and ONE-HALF terms. Six sample-studies are undertaken, each of a duration of approximately NINE weeks.

Section 2A/B: Course Work Topics
Each candidate will prepare up to FIVE national and inter-European topic studies. Each study should be carried out over a period of approximately NINE weeks, during which THREE 40-minute lessons (or equivalent) per week should be allocated. These studies should be timetabled so as to be contemporaneous with the studies in Section 1C, lasting over a total period of FOUR and ONE-HALF terms.

European Visits and Exchanges
It is envisaged that ALL candidates will be given the opportunity to make an extended (at least ONE week) visit to the country whose language they have studied.

There will be no specific testing or assessing of this part of the course. It is hoped, however, that candidates will make use of the information and experience collected during such a visit in choosing their coursework topics.

Section 1: The Compulsory Common Core

Section 1A. *The Study of One European Language*

One foreign language should be studied. Since this language will normally be French, a suitable course in French has been devised, and will be issued as a separate booklet with associated tapes. Similar courses in German or other European languages would, of course, also be acceptable.

The course is designed as much as is linguistically possible for all ranges of ability. To bring it within the range of pupils with limited aptitude for languages, it is, however, the teaching method which is of most importance. The course is not graded from start to finish. The standard remains constant with a continual re-use of a limited number of structures within realistic situations. The aim is *not* necessarily to elicit strictly accurate spoken French. If pupils of limited language aptitude are to follow this course, this basic precept must be accepted.

The basic aim is:
  (i)   to promote understanding of the main elements of conversation met within situations encountered on a visit to the country, e.g. meals, shops, money, etc.;
 (ii)   to express simple requirements orally and to write simple communications to French acquaintances;
(iii)   to get to know background information of a linguistic nature essential to the understanding of a foreign country e.g. road signs, menus, etc.

More able pupils should be able to acquire enough basic French to enable them to enthuse a little in everyday situations, and to ask important questions as politely as possible within their linguistic restrictions. Any French which non-linguistic pupils acquire should be regarded as a bonus.

Above all, any French uttered by pupils should not be interrupted or corrected in any way, however ungrammatical the construction used.

For all pupils the course will provide opportunities for topic work.

Each unit provides a number of suitable suggestions for assessment. The final testing of this part of the syllabus is to be in both the written and oral modes.

Candidate's written work will be almost all in English, and concerned with comprehension of the foreign language. The detailed means of assessment will be set out in the accompanying booklet.

Section 1B. *The Changing Map of Europe*

(a)   The location of main relief and drainage features; nations; important towns.

(b)   The United Kingdom and Europe: Distance and time-of-travel maps by air and land/sea transport by main direct routes between important centres.

(c)   Cultural influences on Europe: The patterns of distribution of the main racial, linguistic and religious influences (emphasis should be placed on location and only passing reference made to reasons for these patterns).

(d) Europe in 1939: National boundaries. Types of governments (i.e. parliamentary, totalitarian, monarchical, republican). The Second World War (allied, axis and neutral states).

(e) Europe in 1945: The final extent of Soviet advance. Political boundaries. The 'Cold War' (origins and effects; NATO and the Warsaw Pact).

(f) Progress towards European unity; the Common Market; EFTA; Comecon.

(g) Europe and the World: Rich World/Poor World (the measurement of Europe's population and wealth in comparison with other 'developed' nations and with the 'underdeveloped' nations of the world).

Section 1C. *Sample Studies of European Societies*
Candidates will study SIX European societies—Germany, Sweden, the Netherlands, France, Italy, Spain.

Each of these societies will be studied using the following common framework:

(a) Introduction:
  (i) The nation in Europe: Relationship to the United Kingdom in terms of times and distances of travel between selected important centres.
  (ii) Location maps: Physical structure, population, land-use, industry and communications.

(b) Family life: Introduction to ways of living; currency and exchange rates; relative costs and standards of living.

(c) Employment and working conditions: Sample salary and wage levels in the professions, industry and agriculture; distribution of labour force in services, industry and agriculture; hours of work; holidays.

(d) Food, drink and eating customs: Main foods and beverages; times of meals; a typical morning and evening meal.

(e) Education: The provision of education by types and ages, in comparison with those in the United Kingdom (e.g. selection, co-education and main curriculum differences).

(f) Sport: The main national sports, games and pastimes.

(g) Government: The main characteristics and functions of Central and Local Government systems; election systems.

Section 2: Course Work Topics

Section 2A. *Aspects of National Ways of Life Within European Countries*
Not more than ONE topic may be submitted from this section, concerned with any of the countries studied in Section 1C.

(a) *Regional Studies—Landscape and Ways of Life*
  The study of one important region or city under the headings:
  (i) Location.
  (ii) Outstanding historical features of the contemporary landscape and ways of life.

    (iii) Present economic, social and political importance.
    (iv) Regional characteristics of community life and customs.

(b) *A Family*
The study of one family group based on correspondence and/or a visit.
    (i) A typical week in the life of the family.
    (ii) The father at work.
    (iii) The domestic role of the mother.
    (iv) The children at school and in their outside activities.
    (v) The weekend.
    (vi) The annual holiday.

(c) *Food, Beverages and Menus*
The study of the eating, drinking and culinary customs of the country or a region within the country.
    (i) Foodstuffs in the basic diet.
    (ii) Speciality foods and beverages.
    (iii) Sample meals and menus (including the preparation of a main meal for which a 'log-book' type account is kept).
    (iv) Cooking methods and kitchen equipment.
    (v) Table laying and serving utensils.

(d) *Topical Events and Problems*
The study of ONE important economic, social, political or environmental event or problem occurring during the period of study. A suggested scheme of work might include:
    (i) The maintaining of a 'log-book' type account of the chronological course of development of the event or problem.
    (ii) The presentation of news accounts and visual material in a folder or file.
    (iii) The preparation and delivery of an oral account of the significance of the event or problem.

(e) *The Nation's Music*
The study of a nation's tastes in music and music-going.
    (i) The 'pop' music scene compared with that in Britain. The Eurovision Song Contest.
    (ii) Famous composers and their music.
    (iii) Opera and ballet and their place in the life of the country.
    (iv) Folk music, songs and dances in the country.

Section 2B. *Inter-European Studies*
Candidates should submit a minimum of TWO of the following course work topics. The detailed content is a suggested approach.

(1) *Energy: The changing pattern of energy use and its influence on social development*
    (a) Comparison of heating and motive power in different countries. Reference to situation in United Kingdom.
    (b) The coalfields—distribution. Example—the Ruhr: changes occurring. (Reasons for the decline in coal consumption and effects on coalfields. Refer to situation in Britain.)

    (c) The discovery of oil and natural gas.
        (i) Resulting changes.
       (ii) Transporting oil and gas.
           Examples: Gas in the Netherlands.
                    Oil and gas in Germany.
                    The Saharan oil and gas and how it is being transported to markets in Europe.
                    The North Sea strike and its effects.
                    Methane gas transport to British Isles.

    (d) Development of water resources for electricity. Examples — The Rance scheme in Brittany.

    (e) Nuclear power. What conditions are required in setting-up a nuclear station; the nuclear power stations in Britain; the Swedish developments; the Euratom policy of the EEC.

(2) *Transport: Changes occurring in transport and their influences on social conditions*
    (a) How one gets from this country to various places in Europe and how to prepare oneself for the journey.
    (b) Advantages and disadvantages of various ways of getting there.
    (c) Railways: Effects of electrification. Effects of political boundaries.
    (d) Tunnels: New developments in Alpine countries. The 'Chunnel'.
    (e) Motorways: German Autobahnen. Italian autostrada. The Europa routes. Advantages and disadvantages of motorways.
    (f) Navigable waterways: Changes occurring on Rhine-Rhone.
    (g) Ports: Ferry services from Britain to Europe. Container services. New super ports: Europort, Antwerp, Marseille.
    (h) Air transport: Concorde. Eurobus jet. London's third airport.

(3) *Tourism*
    (a) Why go abroad?
    (b) Where to go: Playgrounds of Europe — Mediterranean — Adriatic coastline — Switzerland/Austria — Nordic countries.
    (c) How to go and when to go: Package tours — camping — off-season — various ways of getting there.
    (d) Tourism in the economies of two selected countries — Spain — Italy — Yugoslavia — Switzerland.

(4) *Agriculture: Sample studies of farming in Europe*
    (a) A Danish co-operative farm — how the co-op principle and close government supervision ensures the continuing prosperity of the Danish farmer. A typical day and year.
    (b) A peasant farm in Brittany — a typical day and year. How farm consolidation programmes affect the typical family. How agricultural prices negotiated in the other Common Market countries affect the farmer.
    (c) Olive cultivation in Mediterranean Spain — a typical day and year. The Hacienda. Landless labourers. The effects of modernisation — crop diversification and mechanization.
    (d) A fjord farm in Norway — a typical day and year. The problems of a poor environment.

(5) *Industry: The changing patterns of industry in Western Europe*
   (a) The heavy industrial regions of the EEC and how they are being affected by the policies of the Coal and Steel Community.
   (b) The shift of heavy industry to the coast. Examples—Europort, Dunkirk, Marseille.
   (c) New sources of power—the dispersal of industry based on increased use of electric power.
   (d) The influence of large centres of population as an attraction for light industry.
   (e) Specialized industry based on technical knowledge—Examples—Switzerland, Bavaria and the French Jura.

(6) *Education*
   A comparison of the typical daily routine, school work and prospects of school children of several selected countries, with special reference to the exchange areas.
   (a) The course of a typical child's education: Infant, Primary, Secondary, Further Education, showing:
      (i)   ages at which changes are made;
      (ii) whether there is selection and special schooling;
      (iii) examination system;
      (iv) private and religious schooling;
      (v)   co-educational or not.
   (b) The course of a typical child's day and curriculum—comparison of timetables and available choices noticing especially: sports, languages learnt, religion, practical subjects.
   (c) State influence—control of curriculum and permitted flexibility; system of payment for schools, employment of teachers.
   The candidate should examine his own school system and compare it with the school system in his country of visit. He should select at least one other country outside the other five studied in Section 1C.

(7) *Man on the Move*
   The study of various inter-European migrations of man and their causes. A suggested study approach may be:
   (a) Those who continuously move:
      (i)   by choice—tramps, gypsies;
      (ii) by the nature of the job—entertainers, cattle drovers, long distance lorry drivers.
   (b) Those who are short term/seasonal movers:
      (i)   agricultural workers crossing frontiers for harvesting;
      (ii) other movements—visiting lecturers, construction workers, overseas advisers.
   (c) Migrants for permanent settlement:
      (i)   Economic causes—workers for international companies or other international institutions; migratory labour (Italians to Switzerland; Turks to West Germany); West Indians/Asian immigration into Britain, Indonesians into Netherlands.
      (ii) Enforced movements—refugees from eastern Europe in West Germany.

(8) *Eurocar*
  (a) The 'European' car in comparison with the 'American' car in terms of size and engine capacity and other comparisons.
  (b) National styles of car within Europe.
  (c) Car ownership in Europe—persons per car index; relative costs of cars; influence on working and leisure life.
  (d) Problems:
    (i) road congestion;
    (ii) parking systems;
    (iii) safety and pollution.
  (e) The study of ONE car industry from Volkswagen, Renault, Fiat, British Leyland, to show:
    (i) its importance in the country's economic and social life;
    (ii) its history and development.

(9) *Eurosport*
  (a) The mapping of sports peculiar to geographical areas.
  (b) A study of sports which are peculiar to individual nations—e.g. pelota; ski-running—the origins of such sports.
  (c) Soccer—relative importance in individual countries; number of professional clubs; comparative match attendances; players' and managers' salaries. European competitions.
  (d) (i) Study of ONE outstanding European sportsman or sportswoman;
    or (ii) Study of ONE important European sport (other than soccer).
  (e) Conclusions—general attitudes of European countries to sport as compared with those existing in Britain.

(10) *Minorities*
  The study of different minority groups in Europe, their origins and distinctive ways of life. One group to be chosen from each of the following:
  (a) National consciousness within nations:
    (i) Welsh or Scottish nationalism.
    (ii) The Bretons in France.
    (iii) Republicanism in Northern Ireland.
  (b) Traditional minorities:
    (i) Walloons in Belgium.
    (ii) Basques in Spain.
  (c) Recently absorbed groups:
    (i) Algerians in France.
    (ii) Indonesians in the Netherlands.
    (iii) West Indians/Asians in Britain.

In the spring of 1976 Somerset Education Committee published the Second Report on an Integrated Course in European Studies. This contained new syllabus proposals prepared by the Syllabus Review Committee which reports initially to the Somerset Standing Committee on European Studies.

In the Second Report two alternative approaches to the syllabus are elaborated: Syllabus A is a single award scheme where candidates will receive a one subject CSE grade on completion of a two year course; Syllabus B is also for a two year course but at the end of the course pupils will receive CSE grades for two subjects.

There are three components in Syllabus A: a common core of six contemporary European topics, e.g. 'Towards European Unity' and 'New Industry for Old'; a language study which might be French, German or Spanish; course work in which pupils would prepare three projects, one linked to the nation whose language the pupil is studying and the other two focusing on inter-European themes.

For Syllabus B there are also three components: a common core of ten topics; a study of a society and its language, or two societies and two languages drawn from France, Spain or Germany; four projects as course work of which three should be on inter-European themes.

In addition to producing the syllabus outlines which have been used for a Group Mode 3 course in association with the South Western Examinations Board the Standing Committee, led by Roger Clay and Barrie King, has been active in promoting the Somerset 'Resources for Learning Project' which has, in association with commercial publishers, produced a variety of teaching materials to help teachers engaged in developing European Studies courses.

3 The Ordinary Alternative Level Syllabus in European Studies examined by the Associated Examining Board for the General Certificate of Education

Candidates will be entered for examination at GCE OA level for the first time in the summer examinations of 1977. This is the first examination in European Studies to be organized by a GCE Board. In granting permission for the whole of the syllabus to be published here the Associated Examining Board emphasized that teachers intending to enter candidates after 1977 should verify by reference to the Board whether any changes have been made to the syllabus.

THE ASSOCIATED EXAMINING BOARD
for the General Certificate of Education

SYLLABUS IN EUROPEAN STUDIES
ORDINARY ALTERNATIVE LEVEL

European Studies are concerned with the relationships that exist in Europe and with the background to the relationships. The syllabus is designed to enable teachers to bring out both the common threads in the experience of Europeans and the diversity that exists and is likely to continue. The syllabus should lead to an understanding both of the tendency towards integration and co-ordination and the desire to preserve national and regional identity.

The syllabus aims at an understanding of Europe today based on a knowledge of its institutions, and of the conditions, events and processes that have led to the creation of these institutions. At the same time consideration should be given to the limits on the influence and effects of institutions and to the spheres of individual expression and choice. Understanding of contemporary Europe demands a background knowledge of recent history; of economic resources; of political organization and ideologies; and of the cultural legacy of Europe.

The syllabus is intended to cover the whole of Europe, but it is understood that the range of material available and the greater ease of arranging visits may well result in a primary emphasis on Western Europe. At the same time events in Eastern Europe have affected institutions and policies in Western Europe and vice versa, whilst comparisons between the two are often illuminating. It is therefore reasonable to expect more detailed reference to countries outside Eastern Europe with more general reference to Eastern Europe. Students should realize that relationships with the rest of the world affect developments in Europe.

It is not intended that the syllabus and the examination papers shall stress exclusively factual recall, but that candidates shall understand the current state of Europe, recognize relationships that exist, and perceive factors that have caused evolution, change and modifications, and that may do so in the future. The state of Europe is fluid and likely to remain so. The syllabus cannot, therefore, be so rigid that it allows no scope for change.

The syllabus gives students the opportunity to integrate their experiences and learning in this country, both inside and outside the classroom, and to enrich these with visits to Europe, the reception of visitors from Europe, with books, films, periodicals, television and radio programmes. Students whose knowledge of a foreign language is insufficient to allow them to read contemporary literature in the original should read literature relevant to the syllabus in translation.

The syllabus is conceived on the basis of a two-year course in which two or three hours per week are devoted to the subject. The treatment cannot, therefore, be both extensive and detailed. The syllabus combines a broad descriptive treatment of the political, economic, cultural and social scene in Europe, together with scope for a study in greater depth in the coursework. Some of the questions will be framed to allow candidates to refer for illustration of their answers to two or three countries, whilst others may be set on a regional basis.

An examination paper of three hours' duration will be set, carrying 70% of the marks. A choice of questions will be offered. Questions may be set in essay-form, or as structured questions calling for a succession of short answers, or may call for the interpretation of documents, maps, statistics, visual material.

During the course candidates will be required to complete two units of work, which may take the form of an extended essay or a project. The units need not consist entirely of written work, but may incorporate illustrations, photographs, charts, diagrams, tape-recordings where appropriate, but a written section explaining the significance of the material presented will normally be required. The units should not be compilations from existing sources, but should include an element of enquiry or evaluation by the candidate. Part or all of the illustrative material may be presented in a European language or European languages. Where necessary, the content and significance of the material should be explained in English. Candidates may choose their own subjects for these units in consultation with their teachers or tutors, who will submit proposals to a moderator for approval. The units will carry 30% of the total marks, and will be marked by the tutor and moderated by the moderator. The Board will appoint a moderator to each centre or group of centres entering candidates for the examination. Grades cannot normally be awarded to candidates who have not completed both parts of the examination, i.e. the units of course work and the final examination. The examination will be available in the summer series only.

SYLLABUS

Section A

The emergence of contemporary Europe

Factors that have influenced the development of modern Europe including historical, geographical, political and socio-economic, e.g. the effect of two world wars on the map of Europe; the growth of national aspirations; Communism, Fascism, social democracy, totalitarianism in modern Europe; the development of political, economic, religious, and cultural groupings and relations; the distribution of resources in Europe; the impact of technology and scientific progress.

Section B

Europe today

1   Political, military, and economic institutions—neutral and unaligned countries.
2   Current problems in Europe, e.g.
   (i)   The limits of sovereignty.
   (ii)   Movement towards, and obstacles to political unity.
   (iii)   Preservation of identity in small nations, regions, linguistic groups, religious communities, etc.
   (iv)   The environment and pollution as international problems.
   (v)   The different forms and the nature of democracy.
   (vi)   Standards of living—poverty amidst affluence.
   (vii)   External relations with the Middle East, America, Japan, Africa.
   (viii)   The individual and authority.
   NB—Questions will not be limited to these specific topics, and it is expected that candidates will keep in touch with current problems.

Units of course work

The student will complete for assessment by the tutor, subject to moderation by the Board, two units of course work. Examples of suitable areas for enquiry and/or evaluation are given below, but students may choose their own topics provided that these form a part of European Studies. Each unit of work should represent at least ten hours' work, including collection of material, presentation and writing.

The topics selected should be limited in extent so that they are within the scope of individual enquiry or evaluation. Group projects can be accepted only if the individual contribution of each candidate is clearly identifiable.

Examples of course work

Units of course work may be based on political, cultural, social, religious, scientific, technological, and other relevant topics. **The following examples are given for guidance only. It is hoped that topics chosen will be specific rather than general**, e.g. a study of a farmer in Normandy rather than a general essay on European agriculture; a study of the career of Shostakovich rather than an essay on the state and the artist.

General
Anti-semitism; role of women; poverty; minorities; nationalism; 'Resistance'.

Cultural
Novels; poetry; mass media—control of television and radio; Drama; Lit. on current topics such as violence, pacifism, war; Art—expressionists, Corbusier; ownership and distribution of newspapers and periodicals.

Social
Education; local government; housing; social services; legal systems; religion; language(s).

Economic
Planned economies; growth of Germany; tourism in S. Europe; regional problems; scientific and technological changes and their effects.

One unit of coursework should be completed and available for moderation not later than 31 January and the other by 30 April preceding the date of the written examination. Submission at earlier dates will be encouraged wherever this is possible.

4   A CSE Mode 3 Course designed by a Single School

This course was designed by a teacher of modern languages who had been appointed to a secondary modern school which had no tradition of teaching modern languages but which was soon to become comprehensive. It is interesting that the course does not contain a modern language component. The syllabus has three examinable elements: course work, a project and a written paper. This is a typical arrangement of a CSE European Studies course. Several teachers contribute to the teaching of this course and they are drawn from the departments of modern languages and geography. The number of candidates entered for examination fluctuates annually depending on the way in which pupils exercise their choice of options when they enter the fourth year.

A MODE 3 COURSE DESIGNED BY A SINGLE SCHOOL

Aims
To study some of the social, economic and cultural features of Europe, as well

as its history and geography, and by stressing similarities in our ways of life and heritage, to make the pupil conscious of being a European.

Objectives
At the conclusion of the course pupils will be
- (a) precise in observation, in recording their findings in a variety of ways and stimulated to seek explanations;
- (b) trained in the use and appreciation of source materials;
- (c) aware of Europe's problems and concerned for their solution;
- (d) conscious of man's changing response to his environment.

Form of Examination
The examination will comprise:
- Part A   **Individual Project Work** (25%)
  The assessment, prior to the written examination, of a folder, prepared over a period (one year) before the examination.
- Part B   **Written Paper** (50%)
  The paper will be of 2 hours, preceded by 15 minutes' reading time.
- Part C   **Course Assessment** (25%)
  This will be a continuous assessment of the work carried out during the 2 years' course.

SYLLABUS
Part A   Individual Project Work
A project intended to give pupils the opportunity to show that they themselves made a study of an appropriate subject in some depth and over a period of time during the two years previous to the examination.
- (a) It will be selected as a result of a consultation between pupils and teacher.
- (b) It will be presented as a folder or loose-leaf file or in a suitable exercise book.
- (c) The amount of work will vary with the subject studied and the nature and quantity of the accompanying maps, diagrams, illustrations, photographs and models.
- (d) The following is a guide to pupils in selecting subjects for their project work.
  1 European sport.
  2 National/regional dances/costumes.
  3 Fêtes, customs.
  4 Napoleon's campaigns.
  5 Role of one country in First World War.
  6 Role of one country in Second World War.
  7 History of army in Britain (or one regiment).
  8 Domestic architecture (one country or comparison).
  9 National cooking and eating habits.
  10 Detailed study of a Roman site.
  11 De Gaulle's career.
  12 Winston Churchill's career.
  13 Foreign elements in population of Chester.

14 Educational systems in four countries.
15 Foreign influences on English language.
16 Development of airlines for national prestige.
17 Farming—compare a British community with one in France or Italy.
18 Venice.
19 Ports: imports and exports.
20 Fashion: French couture.
21 Coal mining or steel industries—compare one area in Britain with one other.
22 Railways: development and decline.
23 Canals—modern uses in Britain as compared with France, Belgium and Germany.
24 Tourism as a source of income.
25 Newspapers and magazines.
26 Concorde.

Part B Written Paper
Areas of Study
1 The heritage of Rome. A brief study of the garrison town of Chester as typical of a Roman military settlement. This leads to a study of the system of roads in Britain and further to the system of communication within the whole Western Roman Empire. An examination of the boundaries of that Empire, with Hadrian's wall as chief study point, to try to show how the Romans were trying to preserve their way of life from the ravages of the Barbarian. A comparison between the Barbarians and the law and order of Roman rule. The legacy of the Roman occupation apart from ruins—towns, roads, legal system, language. Some elementary linguistics introduced.
2 Invasions and immigrations from Europe into Britain and some study of the causes.
   (a) Early invasions after Romans.
   (b) Norman conquest/Bayeux tapestry.
   (c) Smaller arrivals of immigrants: Huguenots, French aristocrats, Jews.
3 Improvement of European standard of living through trade, leading to present day responsibilities to underdeveloped world. Dominance and decline of Europe.
4 More detailed study of history of four capitals: London, Paris, Rome, Berlin. Show how the fortunes of the country have affected the growth and development of the capital.
5 Barriers and communications. Seas, rivers, canals, mountains. Opening up of mountain and coastal resorts as people become more wealthy and have more leisure time. Railways, airlines, motorways.
6 Modern industrial and agricultural development in Europe. Population movement. Big financial concerns and multinational companies. A look at the car industry of England, France, Italy, Germany.

7 European thought: Christianity, Humanism, Marxism.
8 Impact of war and revolution on Europe in more modern times.
9 Brief survey of some cultural points:
England: Victorian era.
France: Louis XIV and the Chateaux.
Italy: Michelangelo, Leonardo da Vinci, Florence.
Germany: music at the courts of the princes.
10 Common Market: organization and aims.

The paper will consist of:
(a) Multiple choice questions to test memory.
(b) Interpretation of a passage from a newspaper—content relevant to modern Europe.
These questions will be compulsory.
(c) Choice of essays. (2 out of 5).
Candidates will be allowed the use of an atlas.

Part C Course work. Continuous Assessment
Course work will include all work done on the course such as class work and homework or work of any other nature carried out in connection with the course.

5 Proposal for a CEE European Studies Course

This course was introduced to a grammar school which will soon become a sixth-form college. It was submitted to an examinations board as a CSE course to be followed by candidates attending the sixth form in the school. Prior to the formal submission of the course to the board it had been the subject of discussion by a group of teachers meeting in a local teachers centre. The school has a tradition of teaching history through individual projects and this explains the emphasis in the examination arrangements upon course work and projects. It was assumed that most of the candidates following the course would already have attained success in GCE O level examinations which would have included history and geography and a modern language.

The course is taught by a team of three teachers, an historian, a geographer and a teacher of modern languages. From the outset plans were made to establish an exchange of pupils with a mainland European country and this exchange has been a most valuable factor in the strengthening of the course. When the examination board began to experiment with CEE courses this course was considered as suitable for examination at this new level and candidates were awarded CEE grades as supplements to the usual CSE grades for the first time in 1975. This course should be seen as an examinable minority time course in the sixth form and as the school converts to a sixth form college the experience of mounting this course should prove to be invaluable in developing the curriculum of the new sixth form.

PROPOSAL FOR A CEE EUROPEAN STUDIES COURSE
Aims
To promote a consciousness of current European problems and realities among pupils; to arouse an interest in contemporary European society so that pupils may wish to participate actively in the development of that society. These aims will be achieved by the use of both objective and subjective modes of examination and by the pupil's involvement in the use of contemporary sources. Information and experience gained by the pupil in exchange visits or other participation abroad may be used in examination and project work.

Part 1
This part of the course will form a common core to the syllabus and will be based on the theme of urbanization in Europe. This will be studied from two main aspects:
 (a)   rural depopulation;
 (b)   the process of urbanization.
The number of countries studied in the 'Core' will be limited to four in order to allow for some depth of study. Comparisons (and contrasts) will be drawn between countries in their approach to such topics as the needs of large numbers of people living together in a confined area, regional policies, new towns, population movements, traffic and environmental problems, problems of areas suffering from depopulation. One country will be selected from each of the following groups: Scandinavia, Eastern Europe, the EEC as in 1972, the Mediterranean (excluding Italy).

Part 2
One of the following options will be chosen as a study area for a project:

A   *The Home*
This will involve a comparative study of the home environment in Britain with that in other European countries. It could involve such aspects as the pupil's own home situation—occupants of the house, construction, furnishings, cookery, prices, leisure pursuits, etc.; the locality—a town plan, schools, shops, recreational facilities, etc.

B   *Leisure and Entertainment in Europe Today*
This area would involve comparative studies on TV, the cinema, newspapers, magazines, etc. What degree of uniformity exists? Are there any national characteristics and creativeness? Sport? Gambling? Holidays? How important are cultural pursuits to the mass of the population? Music, sculpture, art, theatre, novels, poetry, etc.

C   *Welfare and Social Services*
A comparative study involving both state and voluntary aspects. Old age, unemployment, child welfare, health—how are these aspects dealt with in different countries? What are the special social problems of the present age?

A comparison of educational systems: types of school, examinations, universities, and opportunities available.

D   *Working in Europe*

This could take the form of a comparative study of a particular job in Britain and its equivalent in other European countries or a study of a particular work situation as a basis for new knowledge or a study of attitudes to work. Post war changes in the location and development of new industries and the problems created. The role of the trade unions in different countries.

Additional options may be included according to the interests of the pupils concerned and/or the resources available.

For the purpose of this syllabus Europe is taken to mean the land mass and associated islands west of the Urals. Although the core of the syllabus will be limited to the study of four countries, the project will not be limited to any specific countries.

The project will follow a specific scheme written on one of the listed study areas. It will consist of a written account of the pupil's own work which may be supplemented by maps, models, diagrams, literature, photographs, quotations, sketches, etc. and presented in a folder. The project must be handwritten. A list of sources should be attached. The suggested length is approximately 3,000 words, but this will vary according to how the information is presented. An oral examination will be included.

ASSESSMENT

Part 1

20 marks will be allocated for a written examination, 20 marks for course work and 10 marks for an oral examination of the course work. A file is to be submitted by each candidate: it should consist of 6 pieces of work done during the course. These should be dated and should include the following:

an essay using source materials;

an essay written under test conditions;

work sheets or research papers on various topics.

Part 2

50 marks will be allocated for the project.

(Although this course does not include a specific language content it is essential that pupils who have already studied a language be encouraged to make use of available sources in that language and that those who have not studied a language are able to acquire sources in translation.)

List of Useful Addresses

Atlantic Information Centre for Teachers, 37a High Street, Wimbledon, London SW19 5BY

Central Bureau for Educational Visits and Exchanges, 43 Dorset Street, London W1H 3FN

Centre for Contemporary European Studies (Schools Information Unit), University of Sussex, Falmer, Brighton BN1 9RF

Council of Europe (including the Council for Cultural Co-operation), Strasbourg, 67006, France

European Association of Teachers (United Kingdom Section), 20 Brookfield, Highgate West Hill, London N6 6AS

European Communities Information Service, 20 Kensington Palace Gardens, London W8 4QQ

European Free Trade Association, 9-11 rue de Varembé, 1211 Geneva 20, Switzerland

European Schools' Day (British Committee), Mr J. Marsh, Stretford Grammar School for Boys, Old Stone Road, Stretford, Trafford

North Atlantic Treaty Organization, NATO Headquarters, 1110 Brussels, Belgium

Organization for Economic Co-operation and Development, OECD Headquarters, 2 rue André Pascal, 75775 Paris, France

The European Atlantic Movement (TEAM), 7 Cathedral Close, Exeter, Devon EX1 1EZ

Western European Union, Secretariat, 9 Grosvenor Place, London SW1X 7HL

References

Adelson, J. and O'Neill, R. P., (1966) 'Growth of Political Ideas in Adolescence: the Sense of Community', *Journal of Personality and Social Psychology*, 4

Anderson, R. H., (1966) *Teaching in a World of Change*, Harcourt, Brace and World

Berg, H. D., (1965) 'The Objective Test Item', in Berg, H. D. (ed.) *Evaluation in Social Studies*, 35th Yearbook of the National Council for the Social Studies

Beswick, N., (1975) 'Organizing Resources Centre Project: Six Case Studies', *Final Report of the Schools Council Resources Centre Project*, Heinemann Educational Books

Bloom, B. S. et al, (1956) *Taxonomy of Educational Objectives. I: Cognitive Domain*, Longman

Brugmans, H., (1971) 'Europe: themes and variations', *Education and Culture*, No. 17

Carroll, J. B., (1964) 'Words, Meanings and Concepts', *Harvard Educational Review*, 34 (2)

Central Advisory Council for Education (England), (1963) *Half our Future*, (Newsom Report), Ministry of Education, HMSO

Clarke, L. H., (1973) *Teaching Social Studies in Secondary Schools*, Macmillan

Commission of the European Communities, (1973) 'For a Community Policy on Education' (Janne Report), *Bulletin of the European Communities*, Supplement 10/73

Counter, K., (1974) 'European Studies strive to avoid the too straight and narrow', *Times Higher Education Supplement*, 12th December 1974

Crabtree, C., (1967) 'Supporting Reflective Thinking in the Classroom', in Fair, J. and Shaftel, F. R. (eds.) *Effective Thinking in the Social Studies*, 37th Yearbook of the National Council for the Social Studies

Daffern, E., (1972) *European Integration: An Approach for Sixth Forms and Colleges*, University of Sussex

Dalton, K. et al, (1972) *Simulation Games in Geography*, Macmillan

Davies, R. P., (1972) *Mixed Ability Grouping*, Temple Smith

DES, (1972) *New Thinking in School Geography*, Education Pamphlet No. 59, HMSO

Elliott, G., Sumner, H. and Waplington, A., (1975) *Games and Simulations in the Classroom*, Collins—ESL Bristol for the Schools Council

Eysenck, H. J., (1954) *The Psychology of Politics*, Routledge and Kegan Paul

Fenton, E., (1966) *Teaching the New Social Studies in Secondary Schools*, Holt, Rinehart and Winston

Freeman, P., (1973) 'The Study of French Society in CSE Mode 3 Courses', in *Modern Languages and European Studies*, CILT Reports and Papers 9

Freeman, P., (1970) *European Studies Handbook*, Centre for Contemporary European Studies and Centre for Educational Technology, University of Sussex

Gagné, R. M., (1970) *The Conditions of Learning*, Holt, Rinehart and Winston

Gagné, R. M., (1974) *Essentials of Learning for Instruction*, The Dryden Press

Gronlund, N. E., (1970) *Stating Behavioral Objectives in the Classroom*, Macmillan
HMSO, (1960) *Secondary School Examinations other than the GCE* (Beloe Report)
Hoste, R. and Bloomfield, B., (1975) *Continuous Assessment in the CSE*, Schools Council Examinations Bulletin 31, Evans/Methuen Educational
Husen, T., (1974) *The Learning Society*, Methuen
James, C. V., (1973) 'European Studies and the Study of Europe', in *Modern Languages and European Studies*, CILT Reports and Papers 9
Jones, B. L., (1972) European Studies, *New Era*, 53, December
Jotterand, R., (1966) *Introducing Europe to Senior Pupils*, Council for Cultural Co-operation of the Council of Europe
Kelly, A. V., (1974) *Teaching Mixed Ability Classes*, Harper and Row
Kelly, A. V. (ed.), (1975) *Case Studies in Mixed Ability Teaching*, Harper and Row
Kelman, H. C., (1965) *International Behavior*, Holt, Rinehart and Winston
Kilner, G., (1975) 'A CEE Syllabus for European Studies', *Teaching About Europe*, Vol. 2, No. 2, Spring
King, B., (1974) 'The Language Element in the Somerset Mode 3 Integrated European Studies Syllabus and its Relevance to the Less Able Pupil', *Modern Languages in Scotland*, No. 4, May
Knowles, P., (1972) *Course Development in Studies about Contemporary European Society*, Unpublished dissertation, Centre for Educational Technology, University of Sussex
Lawton, D., (1973) *Social Change, Educational Theory and Curriculum Planning*, University of London Press
Lawton, D. and Dufour, B., (1973) *The New Social Studies*, Heinemann Educational Books
Mackinder, H. J., (1913) 'The Teaching of Geography and History as a Combined Subject', *The Geographical Teacher*, Vol. VII, No. 35
Marshall, J. and Hales, L. W., (1971) *Classroom Test Construction*, Addison Wesley
Massialas, B. G. and Cox, C. B., (1966) *Inquiry in Social Studies*, McGraw-Hill
Mercer, G., (1973) *Political Education and Socialization to Democratic Norms*, Occasional Paper II, Survey Research Centre, University of Strathclyde
Morrison, A. and McIntyre, D., (1971) *Schools and Socialization*, Penguin
Neather, E. J., (1973) 'European Studies: the Somerset Syllabus', in *Modern Languages and European Studies*, CILT Reports and Papers 9
Nesbitt, W. A., (1971) *Simulation Games for the Social Studies Classroom*, Foreign Policy Association, New York
North West Regional Examinations Board, (1976) *Mode 3, Regulations and Notes for Guidance*, Pamphlet No. 2
O'Connell, P. J., (1968) 'Bringing Europe into the Classroom', *European Community*, July/August
Schools Council, (1971) Examinations Bulletin 23, *A Common System of Examining at 16+*, Evans/Methuen Educational
Schools Council, (1972a) *Out and About*, Evans/Methuen Educational
Schools Council, (1972b) Working Paper 43, *School Resources Centres*, Evans/Methuen Educational
School Council, (1973) Working Paper 46, *16-19 Growth and Response, 2, Examination Structure*, Evans/Methuen Educational
Schools Council, (1975a) *Moving Towards the CEE*, (pamphlet)
Schools Council, (1975b) Working Paper 53, *The Whole Curriculum 13-16*, Evans/Methuen Educational
Schools Council, (1975c) Examinations Bulletin 32, *Assessment and Testing in the Secondary School*, Evans/Methuen Educational
Secondary Schools Examinations Council, (1961) Fourth Report, *The Certificate of Secondary Education*, HMSO

Scott, W. A., (1965) 'Psychological and Sociological Correlates of International Images', in Kelman (1965)

Shennan, J. H., (1974) 'European Studies as a Model of Multidisciplinarity', *Times Higher Education Supplement*, 23 August 1974

Shipman, M. D., (1974) *Inside a Curriculum Project*, Methuen

Stenhouse, L., (1969) 'The Humanities Curriculum Project', *Journal of Curriculum Studies*, Vol. 1, No. 1

Stenhouse, L., (1975) *An Introduction to Curriculum Research and Development*, Heinemann Educational Books

Tansey, J., (1971) *Educational Aspects of Simulation*, McGraw-Hill

Thorne, J., (1975) 'European Studies in the Southern Regional Examinations Board', *Teaching About Europe*, Vol 3, No. 1, Winter

Wake, R. A., (1971) *The Idea of Europe*, in a reprint from the Yearbook of the Swedish History Teacher's Association

Wake, R. A., (1973) 'Reflections on European Studies, *Trends in Education*, Europe Issue

Walford, R., (1969) *Games in Geography*, Longman

Wheatcroft, M. and Freeman, P., (1972) *Patterns of Teaching about Contemporary Europe in Secondary Schools*, Centre for Contemporary European Studies, University of Sussex

Williams, M. (ed.), (1976) *Geography and the Integrated Curriculum*, Heinemann Educational Books

Williams, M., (1969) Some Developments in the Teaching of European Studies in Secondary Schools, in Potton, M. (ed.), *Europe in Our Schools*, Centre for Contemporary European Studies, University of Sussex

Williams, R., (1969) *The Long Revolution*, Penguin

Index

157

DATE DUE

GAYLORD			PRINTED IN U.S.A